To [...]
&
Michelle,
Enjoy my book!

Paul Hodg

AUTHOR

PAUL HODGINS

DESIGNER

KATHY LAJVARDI

CREATOR

NAUSHAD HUDA

PRODUCED BY:

I like this grape.
VOICE OF MODERN WINE CULTURE

ILIKETHISGRAPE.COM

THANKS!

Paso's a big place, and this book was a huge undertaking. We couldn't have even scratched the surface of our daunting subject without the help of many folks and institutions who generously gave us their time and expertise.

The winemakers and winery owners who consented to be interviewed for this book have made it infinitely more valuable and interesting. As you will see, their passion and expertise come through in equal measure.

Here's a partial list of valuable contributors:

Jason Haas, Partner and General Manager of Tablas Creek

Stanley and Terry Hoffman, Founders of Hoffman Mountain Ranch (HMR)

Anne Valdespino, Orange County Register

Paso Robles Wine Country Alliance

The Wine History Project of San Luis Obispo County

▼

Christopher Taranto, Communications Director at Paso Robles Wine Country Alliance, whose generosity for this project included everything from providing facts, history and insights for each AVA to memorable karaoke nights at Pine Street Saloon and blind tasting at The Alchemists' Garden.

El Paso de Robles Area Historical Society: At least 18 newspapers have been published in Paso Robles since the 1800s, and the El Paso de Robles Area Historical Society has collected hundreds of them on microfilm and digital media. This place is an invaluable source of information about the early days of Paso. Its Virginia Peterson Research Library is open to everyone.

Naushad and Kathy would like to thank their kids Aara and Nouri for their patience (again!) while we were going through the process of this project. Also, a big cheers to the Huda and Lajvardi families for their ongoing support and love.

PRENTICE PENNY

FOREWORD

DRIVE THROUGH

I didn't grow up with wine. I think the only wine I drank as a younger man was white zinfandel, like everybody else I knew. If I looked at a wine label, I wouldn't know why this wine is different from that wine. And I didn't know what all those words meant: terroir, vintage, chardonnay. I found it all a little bit confusing and intimidating. It made wine seem like some kind of insider's club.

Then I went to a cousin's wedding in Paris. It was my first time outside of the country. I thought, "I'm going to Paris. If I don't like wine here, well, then I just don't like wine." It's like if you don't like gumbo after tasting it in New Orleans, well then you just don't like gumbo.

That's what got me started. I took a basic introduction to wine class at a local wine bar that I liked. It was eye opening. The instructor made it super simple to understand what the words on the label meant and explained the characteristics of different regions. He demystified a lot of things for me. The whole experience just made me want to learn more about this fascinating world. I started watching a bunch of documentaries about wine. It didn't intimidate me anymore.

▼

I think many people my age and younger have gone through the same transformation and become fascinated – not just with wine but the culture and science of it. We're not content just to go to tasting rooms and follow our parents' preferences. We're asking more questions, diving deeper, appreciating wine as part of a bigger canvas.

This trend has been amplified by the advent of social media. It connects the world in ways that allow in-depth exploration. Many wineries are active on Facebook or Instagram, and you can see what's happening at vineyards and inside wineries all over the world. The opportunity to really dig deeper encourages the inner geek in wine lovers.

As a result, wine has become more inclusive. When you see athletes and rappers talking knowledgeably about wine, and more and more women winemakers and winemakers of color, that's proof that wine has broken out of its corner. It's now a world where people are more empowered to be creative, ask questions, break rules and take risks.

Books like this give people the confidence and knowledge to take their own wine journey, and they celebrate the new spirit that has made wine a more universal passion. I still get excited when

▼

somebody shatters my preconceived idea of what wine is, or gives me insight into a wine or the area where it's made. After eight years of being deeply interested in wine, I still love that feeling of surprise. It makes me want to explore!

Prentice Penny is an American producer, writer and director for TV and film. His 2020 film, Uncorked, explored a young Black man's determination to become a master sommelier. He is best known as the showrunner for the HBO series Insecure.

DRIVE THROUGH PASO ROBLES

TABLE OF CONTENTS

▼

CHAPTER

SUB-AVAs OF PASO ROBLES

THE
BIG
CIRCLE

▼

CHAPTER

01:

INTRODUCTION
& HISTORY

INTRODUCTION & HISTORY

DRIVE THROUGH PASO ROBLES

Not long ago, the area around **Paso Robles** was an attractive yet sleepy part of the Golden State, a bucolic place midway between Los Angeles and San Francisco that was known for its hot springs, cattle ranches, almond orchards and proximity to Hearst's famous castle.

The region's commercial wine industry, although it stretched back to the 19th century, was relatively minor and underappreciated by the Napa-centric fans of California wine.

Today, Paso Robles finds itself at the center of the wine world's attention. In the last few years, wine tastemaker Robert Parker, Wine Spectator and other influential voices have pronounced it one of the great emerging wine regions of the world and heaped praise on its winemakers.

EACH YEAR I SPEND AROUND 10 DAYS THERE TASTING, AND EACH YEAR THE QUALITY IMPROVES. MAJOR PROGRESS HAS LARGELY COME NOT FROM MAKERS OF CHARDONNAY, PINOT NOIR, CABERNET SAUVIGNON OR MERLOT, BUT FROM A GROUP OF PRODUCERS OFTEN REFERRED TO AS THE RHÔNE RANGERS, SPECIALIZING IN GRAPE VARIETALS OF THE RHÔNE VALLEY OF FRANCE."

- Rober Parker, 2017

▼

Accolades and point assessments keep rising. So do bottle prices. Some would argue that, for better or worse, Paso's era of Napafication has arrived. Others contend just as vehemently that Paso will never be Napa, nor does it aspire to be.

HOW DID THIS DRAMATIC TRANSFORMATION COME ABOUT?

Who are the winemakers that made it happen?

What are the specific conditions of climate, geography and geology that combine to create Paso's distinctive brand of wine magic?

And what challenges await the area as it expands and morphs to meet the wine world's demands?

Drive Through Paso Robles examines those questions while providing you with a comprehensive guide to the area's sub-AVAs, a short look at its history, and interviews with some of Paso's leading winemakers.

Saxum Vineyards epitomizes

PASO'S LEAP TO FAME

Its 2007 James Berry Vineyard made *Wine Spectator's* 2010 Wine of the Year.

Robert Parker was blown away, awarding it a

100-POINT SCORE:

"UTTER PERFECTION, AND ONE OF THE MOST PROFOUND RHÔNE RANGER WINES I HAVE EVER TASTED.

▼

THE CENTRAL COAST OF CALIFORNIA

Like many parts of the Golden State, the Central Coast of California is distinctive in its beauty. From the rugged hills north of Santa Barbara to the picturesque bay that defines the Monterey Peninsula, certain qualities of climate, topography and geology give the area its undeniable allure.

The region's diversity is obvious as soon as you encounter it by car or plane. Bisected by the north-flowing Salinas River, the 614,000-acre Paso Robles AVA, subdivided in late 2014 into 11 distinct sub-appellations, includes rich river-bottom land, white limestone bluffs, arid mesas, corrugated hills dotted with live oaks, and coastal mountains that rise sharply to more than 3,300 feet near Paso Robles.

Rainfall, too, varies dramatically, from around eight inches per year in the eastern extremes to more than 45 inches annually in the west.

In the heart of the region, an area near the town of Paso Robles, a prevailing Mediterranean climate is moderated by one of the largest regular diurnal temperature swings — the difference between daytime and nocturnal temperature — on the continent.

▼

During many afternoons cool coastal air pours through the Templeton Gap, a low point in the Santa Lucia Range, which arches southeast for 140 miles from Carmel to the Cuyama River in San Luis Obispo County, never more than 11 miles from the coast.

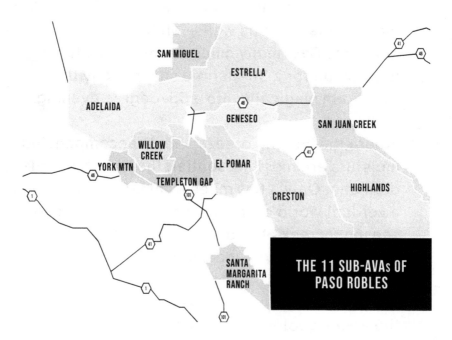

The range consists of many oceanfront ridges that rise directly to heights of 4,000-5,000 feet, focusing airflow through the Templeton Gap.

Marine air enters the gap as the thermal contrast between interior and coastal air increases, plunging mid-afternoon temperatures in certain places suddenly and substantially, especially in the hot months.

This reliable phenomenon cools parts of the area with a refreshing sea breeze. Its effect is surprisingly pervasive, depending on altitude and quirks of geography.

At times the phenomenon is reinforced by cooling air from the north as well — all the way from Monterey Bay, many miles up the coast. It's not uncommon for a 90-degree summer day to transform magically into a 55-degree evening.

Where the cooling breeze and its accompanying moisture are most influential, the effect is visually dramatic. Only a few miles from arid scrubland is a verdant world of thickly wooded hollows and seasonal creeks filled with cottonwoods, lush green undergrowth and songbirds.

This remarkable climatic variation, combined with the area's geological features, make the Central Coast around Paso Robles an ideal spot for growing many types of grapes — an advantage that is finally being fully realized after more than two centuries of viticulture.

In the region east of U.S. Route 101 the maximum daily temperature is customarily higher, which makes that area hospitable to zinfandel and other more heat-tolerant varieties.

▼

The hillier western side of the Paso Robles AVA is distinguished by lime-rich chalky outcroppings and layers, very similar to the geology of France's Rhône region; climate and geology together make the west side especially receptive to southern French red and white varietals and, in some places, cool-climate grapes such as pinot noir and chardonnay.

West of Paso is the 6,400-acre York Mountain AVA, nestled against the eastern side of the Santa Lucia Range. Its lower temperatures and greater moisture are ideal for pinot noir, but its more extensive tree cover and rocky landscape also present vexing challenges for grape growers and winemakers.

Paso's latitudinal location gives it distinct advantages over Napa, Sonoma and other northern California regions. The weather is customarily warm and free of rain until mid-November, allowing grapes more hang time to fully ripen, yet the widespread nocturnal temperature drop ensures excellent acid balance and structure.

The first rainfall of the season is typically about two weeks later than Napa or Sonoma, giving winemakers the luxury of waiting for optimal ripeness.

The Central Coast owes much of its uniqueness to the San Andreas Fault. Running along the east side of the region, this jagged northwest-to-southeast fracture zone effectively forms the eastern border of the entire Central Coast.

It marks the violent intersection of two vast tectonic plates, the North American Plate to the east and the Pacific Plate to the west. The region extending from the west side of the San Andreas Fault to the Pacific Ocean is the only small part of North America situated on the Pacific Plate.

The chain of events that cascade from this constant collision have made the Central Coast geologically, climatically and biologically distinct from the rest of the continent for the last 130 million years.

(One of the most visible effects of this geological collision has been the formation of transverse mountains along the southern border of the Central Coast north of Santa Barbara — the only part of North America's western coastal mountain ranges that runs east-west.)

The area's present climate and geography began to coalesce during the transition between the Miocene and Pliocene periods, around 5 to 8 million years ago. The North Pacific Ocean had developed predictable cyclical temperature patterns and currents that created regular coastal fog and leeward-windward rainfall patterns (wetter on the western slopes of coastal ranges, drier on the east side). The region's Mediterranean climate of hot, dry summers and mild, somewhat rainy winters became firmly established.

During the Pliocene Epoch, the coastal mountains increased their height through tectonic activity. (The Santa Lucia Range is the steepest coastal slope in the contiguous United States.) At the end of that period — about 2.5 million years ago — extensive forests became well established, with Dawn Redwood and other coniferous trees as well as Gingko predominating. These woodlands were interspersed with grasslands and savannas that supported a fecund and diverse ecosystem.

▼

The Pleistocene Epoch, which succeeded the
Pliocene and lasted until recently (about 10,000
years ago), was a time of Ice Ages and fluctuating
sea levels.

The cold, wet glacial periods and dry, warmer
interglacial periods, alternating rapidly in
geological terms, each featured its own indigenous
flora, most of which we would find familiar today.
Gradually, the grassland and coastal chaparral of
the dry climate pushed out the redwood forest that
thrived in cooler times but could not sustain itself at
these latitudes when the temperature warmed. That
climate shift has lasted until the present. Now the
redwoods, which once grew as far south as Santa
Barbara, peter out around Big Sur.

As the last period of glaciation, the Tioga cycle,
began to end around 15,000 years ago, large inland
lakes formed in the flatlands of central California,
including the area east of Paso Robles.

This environment created an unusually rich riparian
habitat that, not surprisingly, became an attractive
place for humans to live. Around 11,000 years ago
the first people entered the valley, drawn by the
abundance of fauna and the rich marine resources
of the Pacific and the coastal river systems.

▼

Given its location on the Pacific Plate, the Central Coast around Paso Robles presents geological characteristics that are strikingly different from most of the state's other wine-producing regions.

ALMOST 50 SOIL TYPES HAVE BEEN IDENTIFIED, DERIVED MAINLY FROM GRANITE, THICK MARINE SEDIMENTARY LAYERS AND VOLCANIC ROCK.

Alluvial fans and thin topsoil deposits often cover shale, volcanic substrate or mudstone. One vineyard block may contain several distinct soil types, presenting both challenges and opportunities for wine producers.

East of the Salinas River, most soil was formed from three large sedimentary formations, the Atascadero, Monterey and Santa Margarita, which date from the Miocene Epoch. These soils contain both calcium and silica.

The area sits atop a gargantuan underground reservoir, the Paso Robles Groundwater Basin, which covers an estimated 436,000 acres or 681 square miles, stretching from south of Atascadero up to San Ardo in Monterey County and from U.S. Route 101 in the west to Shandon in the east.

▼

The quality of the water is consistently good as groundwater moves generally northerly through the basin.

STUDIES IN THE 1980s AND '90s LED TO ESTIMATES THAT THE BASIN CONTAINS MORE THAN 30,000,000 ACRE FEET OF WATER, MAKING IT A TREMENDOUSLY VALUABLE AND COVETED RESOURCE.

It has proven to be vital to the development of the wine industry in the area, especially in the hotter, more arid east side.

IN THE LAST DECADE, EMERGING ISSUES AND PRESSURES AND COMPETING INTERESTS HAVE BROUGHT INTO FOCUS THE ONGING HEALTH AND SUSTAINABILITY OF THE PASO ROBLES GROUNDWATER BASIN.

▼

These challenges are bound to continue as the area develops, more vineyards are planted in recently designated appellations, and overall agricultural activity increases. The Paso Groundwater Sustainability Plan, which will likely place new restrictions on water usage, is currently being reviewed beginning in the state and will be implemented by 2022 if approved.

West of the river, alluvial deposits as deep as 100 feet in places are common. So are the calcareous formations, whose brilliantly white, often crumbling faces can be seen clearly in road cuts and natural outcroppings west of town.

A closer examination reveals their origin: marine fossils are embedded prominently in the rock. Clearly it is an ancient, up-thrust seabed.

Besides the cooling effect of the marine air, Paso Robles' climate provides other characteristics beneficial to grape growing.

Despite the warm summers, variation in average monthly air temperature is remarkably narrow, typical of most coastal regions. Measurements at the Paso Robles airport weather station, just east of town, provide a typical picture: from 47°F. in December and January to just over 71°F. in July and August.

AVERAGE ANNUAL TEMPERATURE IN PASO IS 59.1°F.

The absence of extremes is beneficial to grape growers, of course — with only occasional frosts, no need to winterize and no extended periods of excessive heat, many of the temperature challenges found in other wine regions are far less of a worry here.

Precipitation is also kind to the wine industry in Paso Robles. Patterns are consistent and dovetail perfectly with viticulture's needs.

The rainiest months are December through February (between 2.5 and 3 inches per month on average). The rest of the year is much drier, especially May through October, when rainfall is negligible.

This pattern is well suited to the bathtub-graph theory of vineyard water management, which advocates generous irrigation only at the beginning and end of the grapes' growth cycle and "water starvation" during the middle months of the growing season.

▼

100 CENTURIES OF HABITATION

Paso Robles sits in the middle of a region long prized for its fertility, its benevolent climate and its thermal springs. The first inhabitants, the Salinan and the Chumash peoples, congregated here because of them, developing remarkably stable and egalitarian societies that lasted for centuries and lived in peaceful co-existence. Evidence of their long association with the area has been found everywhere around Paso Robles, especially in river valleys and coastal flatlands.

Archeological excavations around Paso Robles have produced strong indications that this part of the Central Coast has been consistently occupied for at least 10,000 years. The Salinan (whose own tribal name is "Te'po'ta'ahl" or "People of the Oaks") ranged from Carmel Valley in the north to Morro Bay in the south; they thrived mainly in the San Antonio Valley, to the north of Paso Robles. Their 18th-century population was divided into two groups, the Miguelino in the south and the Antoniano in the north.

They were accomplished hunters and had developed a highly nuanced justice system. The origin of their language is in dispute (Salinan may be a part of the Hokan family), but some estimate it to be 6,000 years old or perhaps even more ancient. Sadly, the last native speaker died in 1958.

▼

ALONG THE COAST, THE CHUMASH ESTABLISHED IMPORTANT SETTLEMENTS IN PROMINENT FISHING SPOTS SUCH AS LOS OSOS AND MORRO BAY.

Many Chumash elders claim their tribal name means "bead maker" or "seashell people," evidence of their close association with the sea. They were accomplished boat makers and sailors, and their vessels could venture surprisingly far from shore.

Both the Salinan and the Chumash enjoyed relative prosperity because of the abundant resources of the Central Coast.

The Central Coast natives' peaceful world changed forever in 1769, when a Spanish land expedition left Baja California and reached the Santa Barbara Channel. It was led by Gaspar de Portola, who had recently been made governor of Las Californias.

His appointment was part of a geopolitical chess game: Spain's King Carlos III was intent on establishing a strong presence in Alta California, Spain's northern coastal region, to counter expansionist threats from the Russians and the British.

In a dispatch dated January 23, 1768, the king ordered a series of expeditions to establish colonies and missions at San Diego Bay and Monterey Bay. (The Spanish regarded Californian colonization as a matter of long-delayed destiny. The region had been explored and described by Spanish explorer Sebastián Vizcaíno, who had sailed up the California coast in 1602 and mapped it in detail as far north as Monterey Bay.)

Portola was placed in charge of a four-part expedition organized by Jose de Galvez, the Spanish Inspector General. Accompanied by a group of Franciscans led by Father Junipero Serra, a Spanish-born Roman Catholic priest and Franciscan friar, Portola's expedition left the mission at Velicata on the Baja peninsula on May 15, 1769. The party met with foul weather and bad navigational luck, and many died during the short journey to their first goal, present-day San Diego; barely 100 of 219 men survived.

▼

Nevertheless, Portola was eager to push northward, setting out by land on July 14, 1769 with 63 soldiers, about 100 pack mules and Father Juan Crespi, the expedition's diarist. It took them nearly three weeks to reach the area now occupied by downtown Los Angeles.

From there they headed west to the ocean, following native trails that led to the bluffs above Santa Monica, then turned north. They reached the Central Coast a little more than a month later, arriving in San Simeon about Sept. 13. It marked the beginning of a new era. Almost 170 years after first claiming the California coast, the Spanish finally began settling it in earnest.

Over the succeeding decades of the 18th century, Father Serra established a system of missions, all of them close to (but not on) the Pacific Coast, and each about a day's ride from the next.

He founded the Mission San Luis Obispo de Tolosa in 1772. Today it is an active and well-preserved part of downtown San Luis Obispo, south of Paso Robles, one of two missions in the area. The other, San Miguel Archangel, was established in 1797 by Serra's successor, Fermín Lasuén (Serra died in 1784).

▼

Estimates about the size of the native Californian population in the mid-18th century vary and are based on sketchy sources, but as many as 300,000 people in more than 100 distinct tribes may have lived within the state's present-day borders at the time of Portola's first expedition.

During the mission period (1769 through 1833) and subsequent Mexican and American occupations, their numbers were decimated by genocide and disease.

HANDBOOK OF THE INDIANS OF CALIFORNIA ESTIMATES THAT CALIFORNIA'S INDIGENOUS POPULATION FELL TO 150,000 IN 1848, 30,000 IN 1870 AND 16,000 BY 1900.

Certainly by the mid-1800s, their long-established culture and way of life had largely disappeared.

THE CHURCH BRINGS WINEMAKING TO CALIFORNIA

In California, wine and the Catholic Church are as tightly intertwined as two ancient grape vines. In order to appreciate the many-chaptered history of wine on the Central Coast, it's necessary to understand the role of the Catholic Church in the birth of California winemaking and its survival during some dark times.

Despite his controversial legacy, the state's wine industry owes a huge debt to the father of the mission system, Father Junipero Serra (granted sainthood in 2015) and his followers.

The state's wine industry can be directly traced to the Church's agricultural practices and customs during the mission era.

And if it weren't for Catholicism's need for sacramental wine, California's winemaking industry might have withered completely during Prohibition.

Spanish missionaries and other early European settlers brought the first grape vines to the state in the latter part of the 18th century, although there is written evidence that a vineyard was planted by Eusebio Francisco Kino, a Spanish Jesuit missionary, at Misión San Bruno in Baja California in 1683.

As the mission system crept inexorably north along the Camino Real, the main route between the missions, grapes were planted immediately, mainly for the purpose of making sacramental wine.

Historians have determined that the first vineyard of the mission era was planted around 1779 at California's first mission, San Diego de Alcalá, in present-day San Diego; the premiere vintage was in 1782. Coastal California's Mediterranean climate was perfect for many kinds of southern European grapes, particularly those of Italy, Spain and southern France.

The preferred wine of the time would probably not find favor with many wine connoisseurs today: quite sweet, often fortified, it could be as strong as port or sherry.

Nevertheless it was in high demand, particularly from the Church.

▼

Father Serra complained that the missions often struggled to produce enough wine for the celebration of the Mass.

The grape of choice for the clerics' vineyards, called the Mission grape, is shrouded in mystery. There is disagreement about its origins, although it almost certainly came to the New World from Spain.

The prime candidate is the Listán Prieto, a red grape, which probably originated in the Castilla – La Mancha region. It is genetically identical to the pink criolla grape from Argentina and Chile's red país grape, which dominated New World winemaking for three centuries before the arrival of other European grapes in the 19th century.

Hardy, productive and long-lasting, Mission grapevines produced fruit that was better for sweet, fortified wines and brandy than high-quality dry wines.

Towards the end of the mission era, winemaking grew to become a significant source of income for the Catholic Church in California. Each of its 21 missions had vineyards, although some were more productive than others; the vineyards of Mission San Gabriel were the largest producer of commercial wine.

▼

AFTER THE MISSION ERA ENDED IN 1833, WINEMAKING OUTSIDE THE SUPERVISION OF THE CHURCH GREW IN POPULARITY.

Many of the early winemaking families came from Catholic countries, especially France, Italy and Spain, and were familiar with the processes and rules governing the making of altar wine.

Buena Vista, Krug, Gundlach Bundschu and other commercial wineries of the time undoubtedly provided wine for the Catholic Church, although evidence is largely anecdotal. It was in this era that the Mission grape was quickly supplanted in popularity by other more refined varieties, mainly from France and Italy.

In the latter half of the 19th century, Europe's winemakers fought a losing battle with phylloxera, a vineyard-destroying root louse introduced from America in 1863.

Some historians estimate that 90 percent of European vineyards were decimated by 1889.

▼

The American wine industry flourished because New World varieties had developed a hardy resistance to the disease, since it was indigenous to the region. Benefitting from Europe's loss, California boasted a large wine industry with a global reach by the turn of the 20th century, and California wines were beginning to win prestigious European competitions.

Captain Gustave Niebaum's Inglenook Winery in Napa Valley's Rutherford won gold medals at the World's Fair of Paris in 1889 for its Bordeaux-style wines. California wine was finding enthusiastic markets in Australia, Canada, Central America, England, Germany, Mexico and Asia.

BUT THE AMERICAN WINE INDUSTRY WAS SOON FELLED BY A MAN-MADE DISASTER CALLED PROHIBITION.

Enacted in 1919, the Volstead Act and the 18th Amendment to the U.S. Constitution prohibited the "manufacture, sale, or transportation of intoxicating liquors." Before 1920, the U.S. was home to more than 2,500 commercial wineries. Less than 100 survived the 13 years of Prohibition.

Making wine for the Catholic Church was the principal source of income for many of them. It was fitting, somehow, that the institution that brought wine to California should save it from extinction many years later.

HOUSEHOLDS WERE ALLOWED TO "MAKE 200 GALLONS OF NON-INTOXICATING CIDER AND FRUIT JUICE PER YEAR."

That opportunity created a popular new hobby: home winemaking. Simple kits for creating wine that included instruction books, wine bricks, grape concentrate and raisin cakes became popular throughout the U.S. during Prohibition.

San Francisco alone consumed about 2,000 train-car loads of grapes for home winemaking every year in the 1920s and early 1930s.

▼

PASO'S PIONEERS

The name El Paso de Robles ("The Pass of the Oaks") was recorded in 1828 at a rancho north of the present town where the padres of Mission San Miguel sowed wheat.

After the missions were secularized and opened to private ownership in 1835, commerce began to change the area around Paso Robles. In 1844, Manuel Micheltorena, Governor of Alta California, granted six square leagues, or about 26,000 acres, to Pedro Narvaez (a Mexican naval officer who was captain of the port of Monterey from 1839 to 1844), establishing the Rancho El Paso de Robles. The next year Narvaez transferred title to a retired Mexican army sergeant named Petronilo Rios.

The post-Colonial era started in earnest on Aug. 2, 1857, when brothers James H. and Daniel Drew Blackburn, together with their business colleague Lazarus Godchaux, purchased the El Paso de Robles land grant from Rios. In 1860 Daniel Blackburn became owner of the portion that eventually became the town site of Paso Robles.

▼

In 1864, an attractive mid-sized hotel opened its doors as a rest stop for travelers along the Camino Real.

Its biggest attraction was a bathhouse on the corner of 10th and Spring streets that took advantage of Paso's hot sulfur springs. Within a few years, fans of the "healing waters" were traveling to the area from many parts of the country to seek cures for their ailments and take in the burgeoning social scene.

Paso's history wasn't particularly violent, but it is a footnote to one of the Wild West's most notorious gangs. Drury James, uncle of the famous outlaws Frank and Jesse, was among the town's founders. He co-owned the large La Panza Ranch about 40 miles east of Paso, and in 1868 he purchased a half interest in the town site.

After robbing a bank in Russellville, Kentucky, in March of 1868, Frank and Jesse James sought their uncle's help, hiding out at his ranch until December of the following year.

Jesse also found comfort at the hot springs for lung problems caused by gunshot wounds. He was never recognized in the frontier town far from the scenes of his crimes.

▼

The brothers may also have explored much of the county. Some say that a scratched-out inscription, JES JAMES-1869, was found on one of the Carneros Rocks along the San Luis Obispo-Kern County line.

With the eagerly anticipated arrival of the Southern Pacific Railroad in 1886, the region around Paso Robles became more accessible and attractive to businessmen, ranchers and farmers.

Prior to the construction of the rail line, crops and cattle were usually transported over the Santa Lucia Range and shipped by boat from a pier in Cayucos to markets up and down the coast. The railroad allowed cattle ranches, wheat and barley farms, almond and apple orchards and vineyards to flourish.

A SPECIAL TRAIN FROM SAN FRANCISCO BROUGHT PROSPECTIVE INVESTORS TO THE VALLEY IN OCTOBER 1886.

They were feted with daily barbecues and other festivities in the town's new central public park, established by the Blackburns.

The following month, 228 lots were sold at auction.

▼

In 1889, rapidly growing Paso Robles incorporated as a city. As was the custom for ambitious new American frontier settlements, a luxury hotel was started that year.

When it opened two years later, the three-story El Paso de Robles Hotel was a showy standout in the raw-around-the-edges town. Built at an exorbitant cost of $160,000, it was a substantial structure with more than 1 million bricks, sandstone arches, a seven-acre garden and (highly unusual for the time) a nine-hole golf course.

The hotel's centerpiece, though, was its mineral baths. Paso's hot springs served 32 private bathrooms and a plunge bath that was among the nation's finest.

Over the succeeding decades it became a common destination for some of the most famous names of their eras: Boxing champion Jack Dempsey, President Theodore Roosevelt, writer Adela Rogers-St. John, Phoebe Apperson Hearst (the mother of William Randolph Hearst), actors Douglas Fairbanks, Boris Karloff, Bob Hope and Clark Gable.

▼

Two Major League baseball teams used Paso Robles as a spring training home, the Pittsburgh Pirates and the Chicago White Sox.

Ignace Paderewski visited Paso Robles for several weeks in 1913, seeking relief from arthritis in its mineral baths.

The celebrated Polish pianist, composer and statesman loved the valley so much that over the next two years he bought a pair of ranches a few miles west of town, naming them Rancho San Ignacio and Rancho Santa Helena.

The neophyte farmer planted orchards and vineyards.

COMMERCIAL WINEMAKING ARRIVES

Long before it was known for its zinfandels and Rhône blends, the area surrounding Paso Robles was celebrated for its almonds; indeed, it was the largest single almond-producing region in the world and still produces a significant part of the global market.

By 1920 it was being called "The Almond Capital of the World," with more than 25,000 acres of almond orchards scattered mainly east of present-day U.S. Route 101.

Grapes have been grown around Paso Robles since the 1790s, when they were first cultivated and fermented by the friars of the Mission San Miguel, north of town, and near the Mission San Luis Obispo de Tolosa further south.

It would take several decades for farmers to grasp the valley's vast viticulture potential, but a succession of industrious Europeans led the way.

In 1853, French immigrant Pierre Hypolite Dallidet arrived in San Luis Obispo and established a seven-acre vineyard with some of the original mission plantings; later he added a winery. Dallidet bottled his wine and sold it locally as well as throughout the state of California.

He was probably the first winemaker in the county to make blended wines. His wines are praised in a number of newspaper accounts of the time.

▼

According to an 1889 article in a local paper, the Daily Republic, "Until the last two or three years there was scarcely any wine made except by Mr. Dallidet, who usually made about 6,000 or 8,000 gallons annually and a few hundred gallons of brandy. Wine made from the mission grape and bottled twenty years ago by Mr. Dallidet is now equal to the best Chateau wine of France."

Nearby in Arroyo Grande, Englishman Henry Ditmas imported zinfandel and muscat grapes from France and Spain for vineyards at his 560-acre Rancho Saucelito in the upper Arroyo Grande Valley. He cleared land and planted vineyards by 1879. According to The Wine History Project of San Luis Obispo County, "the wines made from the grapes planted by the legendary Henry Ditmas were always noted for their quality and superior flavor."

The first commercial winery in the region was established by an Indiana native, Andrew York, on his 240-acre farm in 1882. York was surprised that his table-grape plantings in the foothills far west of town quickly produced more fruit than he could sell, so he built a small winery, which he called Ascension. York Mountain, where he established his business, is named in his honor.

Adolphe Siot was born in France in 1863 and immigrated to San Luis Obispo County in 1885. He likely joined his older brother, Peter, who was born in 1858 and had come to San Luis Obispo County a year earlier.

Records show that Adolphe Siot purchased 35 acres near Templeton in 1891 from the West Coast Land Company, and grapevines were planted immediately. Siot employed traditional European techniques for the zinfandel grapes on his hilly land: dry farming and head pruning.

Other immigrants followed suit: the Ernst family arrived from Geneseo, Illinois in 1884 and planted 25 varieties over the next two decades. Gerd and Ilsabe Klintworth began producing zinfandel, muscatel and port in 1886, as well as the region's first white wine; Casteel Vineyards appeared just after the turn of the 20th century.

Even Paderewski got into the act, planting petite sirah and zinfandel on his 2,000-acre spread, Rancho San Ignacio, in the early 1920s. Eventually his efforts resulted in award-winning wines. Despite its size, Rancho San Ignacio was still a rich man's hobby farm. It took a group of hardy, working-class Italian immigrants to finally establish Paso Robles as a serious commercial wine region.

EARLY 20TH-CENTURY ITALIAN FAMILIES GROW DEEP ROOTS

"Paso style" zinfandel was a trademark of the area for decades before Paso became a rising star in the wine world.

Often high in alcohol, intensely peppery and extremely fruit-forward, it was dismissed by many critics as a grotesque distortion of California's emblematic variety.

Others praised Paso's zinfandels as a bold re-imagination of an undervalued grape, and lovers of zin — many introduced to its distinctive qualities through the burgeoning popularity of ZAP (Zinfandel Advocates & Producers) events — flocked to the region, turning Tobin James and other wineries into raucous tourist attractions.

▼

A debate continues to this day about the quality of Paso zinfandel and its importance to the region, even as many local producers of zinfandel have altered their approach to a more balanced iteration of the wine and found ways to blend it creatively.

THE HISTORY OF ZINFANDEL IN PASO IS INEXTRICABLY LINKED TO SEVERAL ITALIAN-AMERICAN FAMILIES WHO MADE IT THRIVE THERE, AND ANY HISTORY OF WINEMAKING IN PASO ROBLES WOULD BE INCOMPLETE WITHOUT ACKNOWLEDGING THE CRUCIAL ROLE THAT ITALIAN FARMING FAMILIES PLAYED IN ITS DEVELOPMENT.

Here are three of the most prominent.

▼

DUSI FAMILY

The Dusi family was among the first large-scale wine grape growers on the Central Coast. Dusi Vineyard was born in the 1920s, when Sylvester and Caterina Dusi arrived from Northern Italy and planted vines near Paso Robles. For nearly 100 years, several generations of the family have grown some of California's finest zinfandel grapes. These days, their coveted fruit is more in demand than ever. Dusi's customers include Turley, Tobin James and other premiere Paso-area zinfandel producers. Since 2016, the Dusis have been producing quality grapes from their Paper Street vineyard, a rugged 110-acre site that is planted to zinfandel, mourvedre, grenache, syrah, clairette blanche, tempranillo, carignane, cabernet sauvignon and petite sirah.

Back when the area around Paso Robles was better known for cattle ranching than grape growing, travelers on the 101 would see a single stretch of vines near the highway. "(Dusi) was the only vineyard you could see from the road in the old days," said Janell Dusi, a fourth-generation member of the clan. She is the owner/winemaker at J Dusi Wines, which operates a tasting room and production facility on the south side of State Route 46 a few miles west of Paso.

▼

Zinfandel was by far the most popular variety planted by the Italians who arrived in the valley and other parts of California in the late 19th and early 20th centuries. The Dusis were no different.

"Our first vineyard was planted in 1925 on the east side of the 101. What did they plant? Zinfandel, of course," Dusi said. It was a popular grape for the at-home "loophole" winemakers of the time who made Prohibition-era wine that adhered to the strict laws of the day.

All the Italian grape growers in those days knew each other well. "My great-grandparents were friends with the Pesentis, the Rotas. They all helped each other. My grandmother played Bunco with Mrs. Pesenti every Monday," Janell said, referring to another legendary zinfandel grower in the neighborhood.

As a kid roaming around the vineyards, Janell always wondered why her family didn't do more than just grow grapes. "Watching truckloads of grapes, all of our hard work, going out the driveway, I often said, 'Why don't we make wine?' My dad and my grandfather said, 'We don't do that. We farm the grapes and sell them.'"

▼

Long before Janell Dusi was born in 1980, the family tried its hand at winemaking when the price of grapes slumped. "In the '50s my great-grandfather said, 'Let's make some wine.' They did that for about 10 years. They had their own label called Dusi Wines. (The label was) bright yellow with a martini glass on it. But as soon as grape prices went back up in '62, they closed the winery down and went back to farming the land."

The '60s were watershed years for the Dusis, Janell said, when large winemakers became clients. "They started selling a lot to Carlo Rossi. Ridge began buying a lot of our grapes in '67. Of course, it was mostly jug wine back then."

Dante Dusi Vineyard, named after Janell's grandfather and planted the year World War II ended, is where she spent most of her time growing up. "My dad was a farmer. It wasn't an option to not help. The farm was our backyard, our playground, our livelihood."

No surprise, then, that Janell eventually fell into making wine. "I asked my grandfather when I was 16, 'Could you show me how to make wine?' I made it in trash cans using cheesecloth for the press. I bought a 15-gallon barrel with my own money.

▼

I entered my first wine competition in '97. I only got a bronze or something, but I was thrilled. After that, I started making one barrel a year. It was always zinfandel."

Dusi considered enrolling in the oenology program at UC Davis, but after visiting the campus she changed her mind. "I went to UC Santa Barbara instead. I felt like I already knew so much about grapes."

She majored in international studies at UCSB but came back to the wine industry immediately after graduation, working far afield in Australia and then with her family's neighbor, Turley Wine Cellars, for a couple of years. "I asked them a lot of questions. Everybody here is so friendly and generous."

Meanwhile, Janell's hobby had become a passion. By 2012, she was producing about 2,000 cases per year under the family label. After a few years she decided to make it official, signing a lease on a tasting room and production facility. The family was thrilled.

"My parents and brother became partners. Sometimes we have four generations working here in the tasting room on the weekend." She smiled. "That feels really good."

▼

PESENTI FAMILY

Frank Pesenti and his sister, Maria, immigrated from Bergamo, Italy in 1914 to join her husband, Pietro, who had settled in Willow Creek, southwest of Paso, around 1910. Frank faced huge challenges: he didn't have a dime to his name and he had absolutely no knowledge of English. He started out working with his brother-in-law, felling trees, cutting them up and selling the lumber.

It took eight years, but finally by 1922 Frank had saved enough to send for Caterina, his fiancée, from Italy. He bought some land in 1923 and planted what every Italian family did in those days: zinfandel.

The winery became commercial when Prohibition ended and it was bonded as the Pesenti Winery, a 65-acre operation located on Vineyard Drive in Templeton.

Quality was boosted in 1946 when Frank and Caterina's daughter, Silvia, married Aldo Nerelli. He had worked at his parents' winery on York Mountain, which they had established in 1917 as the Templeton Winery.

▼

Today, two sons of the founders, Aldo Nerelli and Victor Pesenti, run the winery with Frank Nerelli, a grandson.

TURLEY WINE CELLARS BOUGHT OUT PESENTI IN 2000 IN ORDER TO HAVE ITS COVETED 80-YEAR OLD ZINFANDEL VINEYARD THAT FRANK HAD PLANTED.

Frank Nerelli, who owns Zin Alley Winery on Route 46, is a grand-nephew of Pesenti and has some of the original bottles of zinfandel produced at Pesenti Winery on display in his winery tasting room.

The Nerelli family also got their start in the area, planting a vineyard at the foot of York Mountain in 1917. They hold the distinction of being the first local winery to be bonded following the repeal of Prohibition.

▼

ROTTA FAMILY

Gerome (Joe) Rotta immigrated to the United States from the Canton of Ticino, Switzerland, in 1905. He purchased a 120-acre vineyard and winery in 1908 from pioneer winemaker Adolphe Siot. Gerome's brother Clement arrived shortly later, and the brothers learned the craft of winemaking from Siot.

Joe sold the vineyard and winery to Clement in 1922, two years after the start of Prohibition. Like many other winemakers of the era, Clement survived by making sacramental wine for Central Coast Catholic churches.

AFTER THE END OF PROHIBITION IN 1933 THE ROTTA WINERY BECAME BONDED, AND BUSINESS BOOMED THROUGH THE 1970s.

One of only three commercial wineries around Paso at the time, Rotta sold gallon jugs of zinfandel, aged in huge redwood tanks, for $2.24 (50 cents less if you brought your own jug).

▼

The winery was sold, but in the late 1980s Clement's grandson Mike Giubbini, a firefighter at the time, decided to buy it back.

He moved into his grandparents' old home and began revitalizing the vineyard, largely unassisted.

Ironically, a destructive 6.6-magnitude earthquake in December, 2003 helped his plans: the original winery buildings were badly damaged and Giubbini built a new 5,000-square-foot production facility and tasting room on the original site.

With the designation of sub-AVAs in 2014, Rotta found itself in one of the area's most coveted neighborhoods, the Willow Creek District.

It is heavily influenced by the coastal breeze funneled through the nearby Templeton Gap, and its vineyards in the foothills of the Santa Lucia Range take advantage of considerable soil and geological diversity, including old bedrock, calcareous formations, and younger sedimentary rocks formed during the Miocene Era.

▼

THE MODERN ERA BEGINS

From 1960 to the early 1980s, several men with vision and a sense of adventure proved that many areas around Paso Robles could produce good wine. Some were already seasoned vintners and grape growers; others were amateurs who learned the hard way through trial and error as they went along. All of them faced doubters and reluctant financial backing in an area that, at the time, probably supported more cattle than people.

The modern era of wine production, characterized by greater emphasis on quality and an effort to educate consumers about fine wine, began in Paso Robles during the 1960s, a decade when California as a whole was swept up in the new quality wine movement.

For the first time, college-educated winemakers, respected consultants and substantial financial backing played an important part in Paso's wine industry.

This is also the era when Paso's unique attributes as a wine region began to be assessed and better understood.

▼

STANLEY HOFFMAN

The Adelaida District became crucial to Paso's development into a formidable wine region when a Beverly Hills doctor named Stanley Hoffman took an interest in the area. Hoffman's winemaking hobby, which until then had existed mainly in the basement of his home, became a more substantial pastime when he acquired a large piece of land a few miles west of Paso.

"We had a little 10-acre ranch in Thousand Oaks," Stanley's wife Terry recalled. "We wanted our five kids to know a different life than they knew in Beverly Hills." In 1961, the Hoffmans were presented with an opportunity to trade the farm for 1,200 acres of rolling ranch land near Adelaida Road. "There were just cattle on it then," Hoffman recalled in his final interview before he died in 2017.

At first, the Hoffmans grew almonds. "Then we planted walnuts and grapes." He smiled. "I always had grapes in mind."

This time, Hoffman took his winemaking much more seriously. Soon after he planted his first vineyards in 1963, he hired Napa's legendary André Tchelistcheff, one of the pioneering giants of California winemaking, to serve as a consultant.

▼

Tchelistcheff warned them of the challenges they faced: limited water sources, difficult harvesting conditions. "But he thought it had potential," Terry Hoffman said. "He told us, 'You've got to make your mind up. Is this just going to be a hobby or is it a commercial venture?'" The question gave Stanley Hoffman pause. "I was still a doctor full-time."

The Hoffmans took up Tchelistcheff's challenge, traveling to Napa several times at his behest. "People there were very helpful in those days," Terry said. "There wasn't the competition that there is now."

Still, Hoffman's venture seemed like a long shot to the locals. "There were some zinfandel growers in Paso, but nobody that I know of who wanted to grow French varietals like I did. We were the first." He laughed. "People were not encouraging. They said we were crazy."

But Hoffman's hunch became more of a conviction after a trip to France. "We went to Romanée Conti," Terry recalled. (The Côte de Nuits sub-region is world famous for its pinot noir.) "They were very gracious. Stan noticed that the soil there was exactly the same as on our land: chalky limestone. That was what made him decide."

▼

HOFFMAN MOUNTAIN RANCH, WHICH RELEASED ITS FIRST WINE IN 1972, PRODUCED PINOT NOIR AT FIRST FROM A 10-ACRE VINEYARD, THEN ADDED CABERNET SAUVIGNON AND CHARDONNAY.

Hoffman's sons were both involved:
David was the vineyard manager and Michael
was the winemaker.

"Our pinot was surprisingly great right away,"
Hoffman said. "Everything seemed to thrive here.
And the temperatures and the fluctuations and all
the other things necessary to make a first-class
wine were here."

The ranch benefited from a diverse geological
and climate profile, Hoffman said, producing
good results for pinot, cabernet and chardonnay.

▼

"You could have a vineyard close to Peachy Canyon Road, and you could have an area in the south of the ranch, and they produced completely different styles even though they were within a few miles of each other. In 1,200 acres we had many different climates, different soils."

THE WINERY'S PRODUCTION RAMPED UP QUICKLY TO 15,000-20,000 CASES PER YEAR.

But Hoffman struggled with continuing financial challenges.

"There were no investors besides me," Hoffman said. "We had to sell because we had borrowed heavily and the terms of the loan changed. We just hoped that if enough people recognized the quality that existed here, we'd be all right. It's a risky business."

Hoffman was forced to sell the winery in 1981.

▼

It was a bittersweet parting — it closed several years later — but Hoffman was clearly proud of his legacy. "We had won a place in the pecking order. We were the first to use stainless steel (tanks) and French oak. Our pinot noir did well; it got everyone's attention. So did the cabernet. We sold in Europe and Asia as well as the U.S. and won quite a few awards."

Hoffman's name lives on. His influence is acknowledged by the two wineries that now occupy his former vineyards, Daou and Adelaida.

In 2012, Georges and Daniel Daou purchased much of the Hoffman Mountain Ranch property and restored Hoffman's original winery to preserve a vital part of winemaking history on the Central Coast.

"What has happened here in the years since I started is amazing," Hoffman said. "But it doesn't surprise me.

I ALWAYS KNEW THIS WAS A GREAT PLACE FOR WINE."

▼

OTHER TRAILBLAZERS

Hoffman's success led others to follow his example. As a result, cabernet sauvignon became firmly established as the area's leading variety, a dominance it still holds, to the surprise of many who think of Paso as zinfandel and Rhône country (cabernet currently accounts for almost 40 percent of planted acreage).

On the far west side, Stephen Goldman and his father Max purchased the historic Ascension Winery in 1970, helped to establish the York Mountain AVA in 1983, and were the first significant producers of pinot noir in the area at their York Mountain Winery.

A chemist by training, Max Goldman was a seminal figure in the Central Coast wine industry, and he enjoyed a distinguished four-decade career.

His diligent research vastly improved the quality of Central Coast wine. He was widely respected for his careful scholarship and was an early member of the Wine Institute and the American Society of Enologists, serving as its president in 1955-56.

▼

Max worked with faculty at UC Davis and Fresno State to develop techniques and standards for the California wine industry, and he helped set up the curriculum for Fresno State's department of viticulture and enology. He was also a popular lecturer and writer on a number of subjects pertaining to viticulture and winemaking.

Despite Hoffman's and the Goldmans' success on the west side, during the late 1960s to mid-'70s commercially successful grape growers and winemakers gravitated elsewhere, establishing vineyards on the east side of the Salinas River.

Several east-side winemakers have fascinating stories. Bob Young planted the area's first large-scale commercial vineyard, now known as Rancho Dos Amigos on Shandon Heights. Herman Schwartz, managing partner for a group of investors, planted the 500-acre Rancho Tierra Rejada in 1973 (now known as Shimmin Canyon Vineyard).

GARY EBERLE AND HIS HALF-BROTHER JIM GIACOBINE PLANTED 700 ACRES FROM 1973 TO 1977 SEVERAL MILES EAST OF TOWN NEAR HIGHWAY 46.

▼

Their Estrella River Winery was the largest in Paso at the time. Like Hoffman, Eberle and Giacobine were trendsetters. Against the advice of many experts they established the first large, commercially successful syrah vineyard in California, proving that the Paso region held promise for Rhône wines. Their vineyard was the beginning of Paso's highly successful exploration of south-of-France varieties.

During the 1980s, several winemakers cemented Paso's reputation as a place where wine could be made that was both widely popular and critically laudable. Kenneth Volk, original president of the Paso Robles Grape Growers Association, founded Wild Horse Winery and Vineyards in 1981 when he was just 24, expanding it into one of the area's biggest wineries (from 600 to almost 200,000 cases in 22 years). Jerry Lohr, a pioneer in the sustainability movement, has been making wine since 1971.

Lohr recognized the potential of Paso early in his career and began planting there in the mid 1980s. Justin Baldwin purchased 180 rolling acres northwest of Paso Robles in 1981 and achieved considerable acclaim beginning in the early 1990s with his Bordeaux-style blends.

▼

These men were instrumental in Paso's emergence into the world of high-volume winemaking and aggressive marketing.

Tensions between smaller and larger winemakers surfaced for the first time during this era as Paso Robles began its long, halting transformation from sleepy farm-to-market town to a wine country way station with restaurants, hotels and other amenities designed to serve well-heeled tourists.

A GAME-CHANGING MOMENT CAME IN 2000, WHEN JUSTIN VINEYARDS & WINERY'S 1997 ISOSCELES, A BLEND OF CABERNET SAUVIGNON, CABERNET FRANC AND MERLOT, WAS NAMED ONE OF THE TOP 10 WINES IN THE WORLD BY *WINE SPECTATOR*.

That recognition quickly altered outside perceptions of Paso Robles and led to changes in the way the area presented itself to the world.

▼

FINDING ITS OWN WAY
TO GREATNESS

Within the last 20 years, a group of winemakers — some under 40, some a little older, but all of them united by a spirit of determined iconoclasm — have shown that the area around Paso Robles can be fertile ground for daring and often counterintuitive experimentation.

Of course, from the beginning of the modern wine era Paso has been known as a place that tolerated and even encouraged unorthodox thinking. "I came here because I was frankly tired of the regulations and the expectations back home. They can wear a man down," said Frenchman Stephan Asseo, whose L'Aventure Wines was cited by Robert Parker as one of the area's best in his unreservedly enthusiastic 2007 assessment of Paso.

The area around Paso Robles is populated by many winemakers who pulled up stakes in Europe or Northern California to re-establish their careers in a part of the world where the rules are more relaxed.

▼

Some vintners, such as Christian Tietje, a creative wine innovator who made his reputation at Cypher Winery, have been known to throw a dozen or more wildly contrasting grapes into their eccentric blends, including varieties that seldom make a friendly handshake.

Others, such as Eric Jensen of Booker Wines, eschew oak completely in favor of concrete tank fermentation. Andrew Jones of Field Recordings finds "orphan" vineyards — abandoned or neglected for years — and coaxes their under-appreciated grapes to unexpected heights.

These vintners share certain characteristics besides a tendency to ignore winemaking's age-old laws: a deep understanding of the geology and micro-climate of their land; a knack for blending seemingly incompatible varieties in ways that produce a surprising and powerful synergy; and a preference for keeping things small, even after achieving enviable (sometimes worldwide) acclaim.

Their wines epitomize the Paso style.

As success has brought attention and accolades to Paso, extremely wealthy foreign and domestic investors have arrived on the scene, and their plans and visions have created grand possibilities, acts of generous stewardship, some controversy and, at times, tension.

These men and women have tremendous power to shape not only a vital industry but dictate future patterns of economic development along a part of the coast that until relatively recently has known hardship and even poverty. Will their vision turn Paso into a uniquely attractive region in which winemaking is a catalyst for more sweeping, systemic change, or are they content to serve their own interests over the community's? Only time will tell.

Among the most prominent of the deep-pockets investors: Richard Niner, who made his fortune investing in turnaround companies over three decades, became interested in Paso in 1996 after buying a manufacturer of sunglasses in San Luis Obispo.

He bought the 224-acre Bootjack Ranch in 2001 and has expanded his investment and land holdings substantially since then.

▼

Niner made no secret of his desire to be one of Paso's largest producers — he constructed a gargantuan tasting room on Highway 46 with a commercial kitchen, restaurant and adjoining banquet hall. In another part of the valley Niner built a processing facility that can handle hundreds of thousands of cases per year. But since Niner's son Andy took over as the company's president, the winery's ambitions have become more focused on quality than size — a concession, perhaps, to the local pushback that greeted Niner's initial plans.

Swiss-born Hansjörg Wyss, founder of Halter Ranch Vineyard, made his fortune in medical devices; Forbes listed him as the world's 121st-richest person in 2010. In Paso, though, Wyss keeps a low profile. He bought 900 acres of ranch land northwest of town in June of 2000; subsequent purchases have increased the estate to an impressive 2,000 acres.

A longtime advocate of environmental preservation, he intends to leave most of the land wild, has created generous wildlife corridors throughout his vineyards, and operates organically and sustainably.

▼

In 2013, wealthy entrepreneur Don Law and his wife Susie opened one of the area's most lavish tasting rooms and wineries in the Peachy Canyon area, among the highest and most rugged spots in the Adelaida AVA. Law Estate Wines, whose original plantings date to 2008, focuses on Rhône blends, and critical praise was heaped on the wines made by Law's first winemaker, Scott Hawley.

The winery is renowned for its unique and ingeniously simple gravity-flow design. The Laws also decided to build the large facility slightly below the ridge top because they didn't want their winery to visually dominate its neighborhood.

Bill Armstrong, owner of Epoch Estate Wines, bought and meticulously reinvigorated some of Paso's most significant historic vineyards and restored the old York Mountain Winery stone by stone, replicating its 19th-century appearance even as he built a modern facility around it.

Hans Nef, a Swiss entrepreneur and engineer, acquired some prime Paso land in 1996 and produces atypical varieties and blends for reasonable prices at Vina Robles.

▼

Denver businessman Ron Denner built a state-of-the-art gravity-flow facility and produces wine from vineyards in 108 cultivated acres adjacent to James Berry Vineyard, one of the most celebrated in the valley. His Denner Vineyards winery is one of the more unusual and futuristic structures on Vineyard Drive.

Daniel and Georges Daou, two wealthy French/Lebanese brothers, have been producing coveted Bordeaux blends on their Westside property, which encompasses portions of Hoffman's original estate and is crowned by a tasting room that looks like a French chateau.

TODAY MORE THAN 200 PASO-AREA WINERIES HARVEST OVER 40,000 VINEYARD ACRES, PRODUCING DOZENS OF VARIETIES, MOST OF THEM NATIVE TO SPAIN, ITALY AND FRANCE'S BORDEAUX AND RHÔNE REGIONS.

Paso vintners excel at Bordeaux and Rhône blends and have long been known as masters of the state's heritage varietal, zinfandel.

Wine industry tastemakers have taken notice; so have deep-pockets investors. The valley is undergoing the kind of rapid economic and cultural transformation that Napa experienced more than a generation ago at the hands of winemakers, investors and wine aficionados.

But among wine professionals and Paso fans alike, there is a determined effort to avoid "Napafication" — the kind of intense development that has characterized Napa's rise to fame and led to what some see as a patrician self-regard.

Many of those drawn to this part of the Central Coast love it because it offers a rustic counterpoint to Napa's high-end consumer experience.

True, big money and corporate interests have transformed this area to some degree, but self-effacement and a low-key approach to wine and life are crucial components of the Paso style — at least for now.

▼

Late in 2014, Paso Robles was subdivided into 11 new appellations:

ADELAIDA DISTRICT
CRESTON DISTRICT
EL POMAR DISTRICT
PASO ROBLES ESTRELLA DISTRICT
PASO ROBLES GENESEO DISTRICT
PASO ROBLES HIGHLANDS DISTRICT
PASO ROBLES WILLOW CREEK DISTRICT
SAN JUAN CREEK
SAN MIGUEL DISTRICT
SANTA MARGARITA RANCH
TEMPLETON GAP DISTRICT

In the following chapter we'll look in detail at this new world of sub-appellations and their effect on the taste profile of the wines produced there.

And we'll suggest an itinerary that takes you logically through this large and complex wine region and allows you to appreciate its diversity and complexity.

▼

CHAPTER

02:

SUB-AVAs OF
PASO ROBLES

A SPECIAL THANKS TO
- Christopher Taranto -
from the *Paso Robles Wine Country Alliance*
for his research and the primary writing
done for this chapter.

▼

PASO ROBLES

THINK OF THE 614,000 ACRES COVERED BY THE PASO ROBLES AMERICAN VITICULTURAL AREA AS A GIANT CIRCLE, WITH THE CITY OF PASO ROBLES ROUGHLY AT THE CENTER.

The circle is divided into four quadrants by two highways: U.S. Route 101, running north-south, and California State Route 46, running east-west. Upon meeting with the 101, the 46 takes a slight southward jog down that highway for a few miles before continuing west.

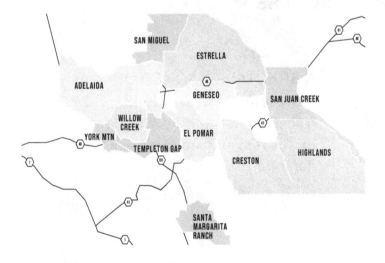

▼

(This description is, of course, an oversimplification. Creston District, San Juan Creek and the Paso Robles Highlands District stretch many miles to the southeast, and Santa Margarita Ranch lies several miles to the south of the other contiguous sub-AVAs.)

We will not include the older York Mountain AVA in our geographical purview, even though it abuts the western edge of the Paso Robles AVA. Its cooler climate, greater rainfall and higher elevation make it distinct from regions of the Paso Robles AVA.

Currently almost more than 60 can be found in the vineyards around Paso Robles; more will undoubtedly appear as winemakers explore the strengths and limitations of their AVAs.

Cabernet sauvignon has long been the most cultivated grape. Merlot, syrah and other Rhône varieties are also popular; so is zinfandel. You'll even find relatively exotic grapes such as vermentino and Alicante Bouschet.

One of the region's great distinctions is its extreme variability of climate and geology, allowing for an amazing diversity of grapes from every significant Old World wine region to be grown here.

▼

If we use the geographical quadrant system as our guide, Paso's sub-AVAs fall into the following groupings, listed here as you might encounter them in a counterclockwise road trip.

NORTHWEST

ADELAIDA DISTRICT
PASO ROBLES WILLOW CREEK DISTRICT

SOUTHWEST

TEMPLETON GAP DISTRICT
SANTA MARGARITA RANCH

SOUTHEAST

EL POMAR DISTRICT
CRESTON DISTRICT
PASO ROBLES HIGHLANDS DISTRICT
SAN JUAN CREEK
PASO ROBLES GENESEO DISTRICT

NORTHEAST

PASO ROBLES ESTRELLA DISTRICT
SAN MIGUEL DISTRICT

▼

THE AVAs OF PASO ROBLES

The American Viticultural Area (AVA) designation is a convenient way to tell the story of a specific winemaking region and convey the common characteristics of the wines that are produced there. An AVA defines a region of variable size, within which certain traits of geology, geography and climate predominate.

Jason Haas of Tablas Creek, one of the region's most literate wine experts, describes the distinctiveness of Paso Robles succinctly: "Paso Robles was the largest un-subdivided AVA in California at approximately 614,000 acres. By contrast, the Napa Valley appellation (which includes sixteen AVAs delineated within its bounds) is roughly one-third the area at 225,000 acres ... (Paso's) vineyard acreage is spread over a sprawling district roughly 42 miles east to west and 32 miles north to south. Average rainfall varies from more than 30 inches a year in extreme western sections to less than 10 inches in areas farther east. Elevations range from 700 feet to more than 2,400 feet. Soils differ dramatically in different parts of the AVA, from the highly calcareous hills out near us to sand, loam and alluvial soils in the Estrella River basin. The warmest parts of the AVA accumulate roughly 20% more heat (measured by growing degree days) than the coolest."

▼

Clearly, the area's size and diversity made smaller, more precise AVA designations inevitable.

The route we suggest isn't a practical day trip for the serious wine fan. It would take weeks of dedicated exploring to do justice to Paso's vast canvas of wines and wineries. And unlike the older sub-appellations of Napa, which have been cultivated for decades, many of these new regions around Paso Robles are just beginning to be explored.

Some contain no wineries or tasting rooms and few vineyards, and their potential is still relatively unknown.

Think of this counter-clockwise itinerary as a path you can join at any point, and a guide to help you make sense of the dramatically contrasting neighborhoods of this large wine-producing region. We have provided detailed descriptions of all the recently designated AVAs, concentrating our efforts on those that have been explored and developed the most.

▼

GLOSSARY FOR AVA DESCRIPTIONS

DIURNAL SWING:

The average daily temperature variance between the coldest and warmest part of the day, measured in the period spanning April 1 to October 31. A wide diurnal swing, especially during crucial parts of the growing cycle, is desirable for the proper ripening of most wine grapes.

WINKLER INDEX:

The Winkler Index, sometimes known as the Winkler Scale or Winkler Regions, is a technique for classifying the climate of wine regions based on growing degree-days. Each day during the growing season (April 1 through October 31 in the Northern Hemisphere) is given a "growing degree-days" number — the amount that the day's average temperature exceeds 50 °F.
The April-through-October total of the growing degree-days determines the Winkler classification. Paso Robles' sub-AVAs fall mainly into Region II or III: II (2,501-3,000 degree days) is best for chardonnay, pinot noir, riesling, cabernet sauvignon, sauvignon blanc, cabernet franc and merlot. Region III (3,001-3,500 degree days) is best for Rhône varieties and zinfandel.

▼

NORTHWEST

ADELAIDA DISTRICT

Adelaida Vineyards and Winery
Alta Colina Vineyard and Winery
Brecon Estate
Calcareous Vineyard
Caparone
Chronic Cellars Winery Inc.
DAOU Vineyards & Winery
Dubost Ranch
Grosso Kresser
Halter Ranch Vineyard
HammerSky Vineyards
JUSTIN Vineyards & Winery
Kiamie Cellars
Kukkula Winery
Law Estate Wines
Le Cuvier Winery
Lone Madrone
McPrice Meyers
Minassian-Young Vineyards
Nenow Family Wines
Oso Libre Winery
Parrish Family Vineyards
Sixmilebridge
Tablas Creek Vineyards
Thacher Winery
The Farm Winery
Tolo Cellars
Villa Creek Cellars
Villicana Winery
Vines on the Marycrest
Whalebone Vineyard
Wild Coyote Estate Winery

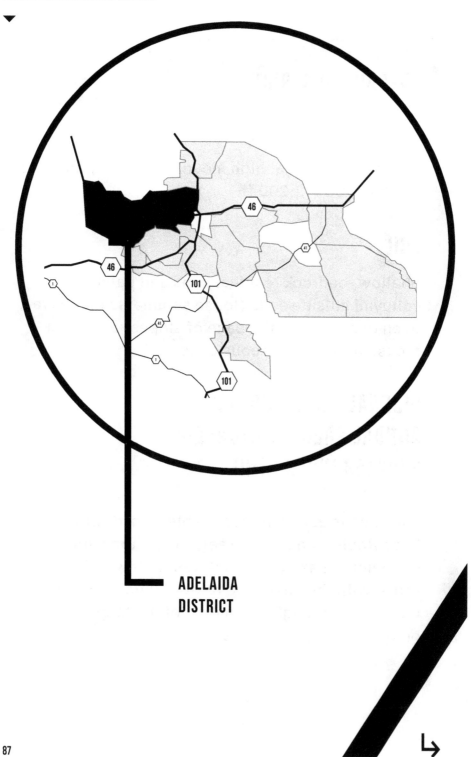

**ADELAIDA
DISTRICT**

▼

ADELAIDA DISTRICT

TOPOGRAPHY:

Santa Lucia Range, high mountain slope grading to foothills; 900-2,200 ft.

SOIL:

Shallow, bedrock residual soils and patchy colluvial hillside soils (loose sediments that have been deposited at the base of slopes) and older rocks; largely calcareous soils.

DIURNAL SWING: 30-40°F
ANNUAL PRECIPITATION: 25"
WINKLER INDEX: II-III

This area is easily approachable from downtown Paso Robles via 24th Street, which turns into Nacimiento Lake Drive just west of town. It then forks, with the left-hand route, Adelaida Road, taking you through the middle of the large and picturesque Adelaida District.

▼

The most northwestern of the 11 Paso Robles sub-AVAs, the Adelaida District occupies approximately 53,100 acres, and it's well defined by its undulating topography, which reaches 2,200 feet in places. The abundant hillsides facing many different directions allow vineyards to be established on sites with alignments that are favorable to specific varieties. Nestled within the southern foothills of the Santa Lucia Range, it's an attractive place dominated by live oak woodland festooned with lace lichen.

The lichen hints at one of the characteristics that distinguishes Adelaida: its abundant rainfall. On average, the Adelaida District receives around 30 inches of rain annually, which is about 20 inches more than some of the drier parts of the greater Paso Robles AVA east of the 101. In exceptionally wet years, vineyards have measured up to 45 inches of precipitation. In dry years, Adelaida might get nine inches or less. Pacific storms can influence the area, and it is often subject to maritime fog. The diurnal variation of the Adelaida District can swing wildly between morning lows of 50°F to afternoon highs of 95°F or more on summer days.

▼

Another distinguishing characteristic of the Adelaida District is its geology. You'll see jagged white bluffs — calcareous formations that reveal the area's history — dominating the landscape. During the Mesozoic Era this region was part of the Pacific seabed, and the chalky rocks are full of the calcified remains of ancient marine life.

This limestone, yellow-white and streaked with crystallized calcite, is often used to build stone walls and structures throughout the area. Adelaida's calcareous soil retains water but distributes it evenly, allowing moisture to penetrate deep into the ground. It encourages vines to sink their roots deeply as they seek hydration during the hot season. Limestone helps to neutralize acids in the soils as well.

There is a modest maritime influence from the Pacific Ocean as the warm air of the Paso Robles area rises, mixing with the cool moist air that pours through the Templeton Gap and often drawing in fog that will roll out of Estero Bay to the west. Further south of the Adelaida District, the Templeton Gap District receives consistently stiff winds. In Adelaida, these winds are less dynamic but retain significant cooling power.

▼

The Adelaida District has the highest average elevation of all the sub-AVAs at 2,200 feet but shares its geology, diurnal temperature swings, and other attributes with its neighboring AVAs. Growers in the Adelaida District have always taken advantage of these circumstances, leading to some exceptional wines.

Surprisingly, more than 88% of the grapes produced in the Adelaida District are cabernet sauvignon. The remainder are mostly Rhône varieties.

Two visionary men dominate the history of this AVA. (For more on Paderewski, see pages 46 and 49.) World-famous pianist, composer and politician Jan Ignacy Paderewski purchased land in the region in February 1914. Subsequent purchases eventually gave him a 2,864-acre ranch about three miles from east to west and four miles north to south. He planted petite sirah and zinfandel on his Rancho San Ignacio vineyard in the Adelaida area.

In the mid-1960s, Los Angeles cardiologist Dr. Stanley Hoffman began planting vines on his 1,200-acre ranch in Adelaida District. (For more on Hoffman see pages 61-65).

▼

His Hoffman Mountain Ranch Winery was the first modern commercial winery in the area. In 1973, famed winemaker and viticulturist Andre Tchelistcheff came to Paso Robles at Hoffman's request.

Tchelistcheff said of the winery:

"LOVE, DEVOTION, AND SELF-SACRIFICE ARE VERY RARE IN THIS DAY, BUT THEY ARE NEEDED TO MAKE GREAT WINES, AND THE HOFFMAN BOYS (STANLEY AND HIS TWO SONS, WHO WORKED WITH HIM) HAVE THESE QUALITIES."

Tchelistcheff called HMR Vineyards "a jewel of ecological elements."

▼

NORTHWEST

PASO ROBLES WILLOW CREEK DISTRICT

Booker Vineyard and Winery
Caliza Winery
Changala Winery
Clos Solène
Copia Vineyards and Winery
Croad Vineyards
Dark Star
Denner Vineyards
Donati Family
Dover Canyon Winery
Dunning Vineyards Estate Winery
Ecluse Wines
Four Lanterns Winery
Fulldraw
Guyomar
Hoyt Family Vineyards
Hunt Cellars
Jack Creek Cellars
Jada Vineyard & Winery
L'Aventure
Ledge Vineyards
Linne Calodo Cellars
Michael Gill Cellars
Midnight Cellars
Miles Garrett Wines
Niner Wine Estates
Opolo Vineyards
Paix Sur Terre Wines
Paso Port
Pelletiere Estate Vineyard and Winery
Per Caso

Proulx Wine
Rangeland
Red Soles Winery
Robert Hall Winery
Rotta
Saxum Vineyards
Serrano Wine
Sextant Wines
Shale Oak Winery
TH Estate Wines
Tooth & Nail WInery
Torrin
Turley
Venteux Vineyards
Volatus
Willow Creek Wine Co.

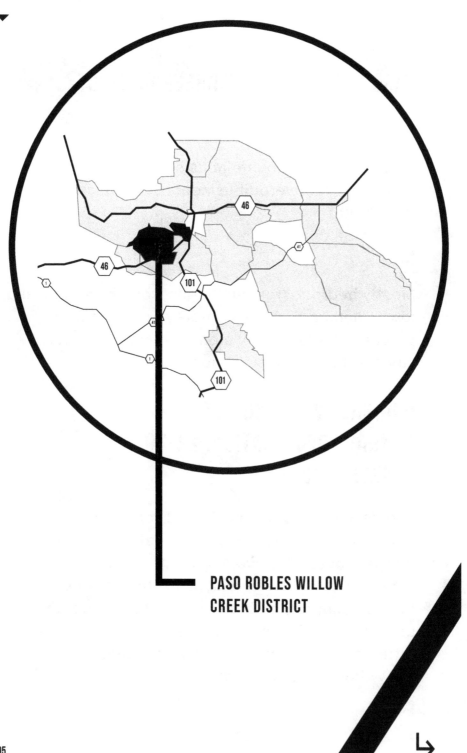

**PASO ROBLES WILLOW
CREEK DISTRICT**

▼

PASO ROBLES WILLOW CREEK DISTRICT

TOPOGRAPHY:

High-elevation mountainous bedrock slopes across the more erodible Monterey Formation. 960-1,900 ft.

SOIL:

Mostly bedrock (residual) soils from the middle and lower members of the Monterey Formation; patches of alluvial soil along streams, largely calcareous loams to clay loams.

DIURNAL SWING: 20-30F
ANNUAL PRECIPITATION: 24-30"
WINKLER INDEX: II

The Paso Robles Willow Creek District and Templeton Gap District come together like complex puzzle pieces. The two AVAs share similar histories as well as very dynamic boundaries, and both sit squarely on the Highway 46 corridor that ushers in the Templeton Gap effect. Where they differ is in the dramatic topography that defines the Willow Creek District.

▼

In the early 1900s, when the Paso Robles region was encouraging settlers to move to the Central Coast, walnuts were the predominant crop in Willow Creek District. Willow Creek's more abundant rainfall made this possible, as dry farming was the only option in those days.

Today many orchards continue to produce walnuts, but little by little they're aging out and being replaced with vines.

Many early settlers in the Willow Creek area planted small vineyards along with grain, nuts and fruits. One of the earliest bonded wineries in the Paso Robles region, The Pesenti Winery, was established in the Willow Creek District in 1934, shortly after the repeal of Prohibition.

Today, the original Pesenti Winery is the home of Turley Wine Cellars, which focuses on wines from old vine, dry-farmed vineyards, many of which are grown in the Willow Creek District and are 80 to 130 years old. One hundred and thirty years old? Yes, according to lore, the Ueberroth Vineyard was planted in the late 1880s by the Tonesi Brothers (it was known back then as the Tonesi Vineyard).

▼

Over the years, time got the better of the vineyard. In the 1960s it was purchased by former MLB commissioner Peter Ueberroth and was renamed the Will-Pete Vineyard, eventually becoming known as the Ueberroth Vineyard.

This special vineyard was lucky enough to have a continuous chain of experts looking after the site — familiar local names like Stephen Goldman, David Osgood, John Munch, Neil Heaton, and Lazaro Morones.

As the story goes, sometime in the early '90s some fruit, around three tons, was going through primary fermentation at Castoro Cellars.

John Munch of Le Cuvier and Niels Udsen of Castoro entered the winery to find the delicious aromas of the Will-Pete Vineyard completely overpowering all the other aromas of fermenting fruit. Today the vineyard is widely regarded as the oldest in the Paso Robles region, let alone the Willow Creek District.

It is farmed and managed by Turley Wine Cellars, who continue to produce a single-vineyard wine honoring this special place and the Ueberroth family name.

▼

The Willow Creek District currently has approximately 1,400 acres under vine with well over 40 wineries, including L'Aventure, Linne Calodo, Midnight Cellars, Saxum, Denner Vineyards, Jack Creek Cellars, Jada Vineyard, Booker Vineyard and Caliza.

The Willow Creek District gets its name from the creek and watershed known as Willow Creek, which runs through the center of the area. Willow trees are commonly found in riparian areas, and because they require moist soils they're usually found along a stream or riverbank.There are probably too many Willow Creeks in the U.S. to count and when the AVA was named, care had to be taken to ensure that naming rights were not infringed upon.

The Paso Robles Willow Creek District is the formal name of the AVA, so named because there is a Willow Creek Winery in New York as well as a Willow Creek AVA in Humboldt and Trinity counties in California. The naming specifically ties it to the Paso Robles area.

▼

Compared to the rest of the Paso Robles AVAs, cool weather persists in the Willow Creek District. Fog from the coast infiltrates the mountain gaps and spills into different plateaus and arroyos, which are often the same paths for consistent ocean breezes.

The Templeton Gap effect also helps to cool more southern portions of the Willow Creek District where the boundary lines blur with its eponymous neighbor, the Templeton Gap District. These winds are far more pronounced than the aforementioned breezes; however, the combination of the two is what defines this region as II on the Winkler scale.

Much like the Adelaida District, you will find limestone all over the Willow Creek District. These easy-to-spot rocks of sedimentary origin are typically a pale sandstone color, contrasting with horizontal lines of crystalline calcite that help give the rock its distinctive striated appearance.

Many extra-large specimens dot the landscape; some have been excavated for farming or development of parcels.

Weather and time round out the edges of these rocks and to a youthful eye they appear to be giant resting turtles, which is how the Turtle Rock winery got its name.

Many of the soils in the Paso Robles Willow Creek District contain not only active lime weathered from soft calcareous shale fragments, but secondary lime within the soil profiles.

These complexes of calcareous origin include the Calodo-Linne complex of alkaline clay loams, the Nacimiento-Ayar-Diablo complex of clay loams, smaller areas of Ryer and Rincon clays and clay loams, and Croply and Gazos clays.

These soils combine to create interesting and sometimes complex growing environments. The Calodo and Linne soils are different in terms of vineyard potential.

The Calodo soil is much shallower and can be more challenging to dry farm, producing low-vigor vineyards. The deeper Linne soils have greater rooting depths and water-holding capacities, producing low to moderate vine vigor.

▼

The soil series that extends eastward from the Paso Robles Willow Creek viticultural area throughout the Templeton Gap District is the deeper Linne series, which is common on older alluvial terraces and benches. All soils in the Paso Robles Willow Creek District tend to be young to intermediate in age with pH values of 7.8 - 8.9 predominating.

The Paso Robles Willow Creek District lies at a relatively high elevation, truly a mountainous area of the coastal range. The slopes become more steep, elevated, and dramatic in the northern portion of the AVA.

Also unique to the region are many conically shaped hills in the neighborhood of Denner Vineyards, James Berry Vineyard, Clos Solene, Booker Vineyard, and L'Aventure.

The Paso Robles Creek watershed, a direct tributary of the Salinas River, runs east-west and originates from the range crest. Feeding the Paso Robles Creek are several smaller tributaries: Jack Creek, which runs north-south at the western edge of the Willow Creek District, and Willow Creek, which sits more to the center of the district and also runs north-south.

▼

These creeks have aided in the sculpting of the landscape by eroding and dissecting the mountain slopes. From the air, there is almost a tree-like pattern that eventually winds its way to the Salinas River.

Hillsides are well covered by the Coast Live Oak, an evergreen that grows all over California's coastal ranges, as well as plenty of chaparral. The Valley Oak, where El Paso de Robles gets its name (Pass of the Oaks), grows majestically in the alluvial and lower-lying areas of the district.

For well over a century, the Paso Robles Willow Creek District has been the home of vineyards, Mennonite families and walnut orchards. It was an area early identified with agricultural potential and as the years and science later confirmed, it yields impressive bounty.

Many popular and burgeoning wine brands from the Paso Robles AVA have made their home in the Willow Creek District, and fruit from the AVA is in high demand. Syrah and Southern Rhône red varietals are strongly represented, along with cabernet sauvignon and viognier. It's alluring even if you're not an oenophile — an area of Paso Robles with diverse landscapes and a timeless feel that is worth exploring for its immense beauty alone.

▼

SOUTHWEST

TEMPLETON GAP DISTRICT

AmByth Estate
Aron Hill Vineyards
Bella Luna Winery
Caelesta
Castoro Cellars
Clavo Cellars
Clesi Wines
Doce Robles
Donati Family Vineyard
Fratelli Perata
Grey Wolf & Barton Family Wines
Austin Hope and Treana
J Dusi Wines
John Alan Winery
Peachy Canyon Winery
Seven Angels Cellars
Summerwood
Victor Hugo Wines
Wild Horse Winery & Vineyards
Windward Vineyard
Zenaida

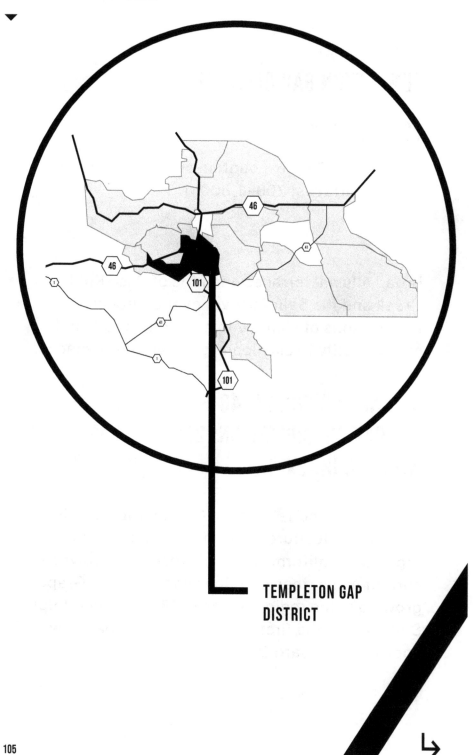

**TEMPLETON GAP
DISTRICT**

▼

TEMPLETON GAP DISTRICT

TOPOGRAPHY:

Santa Lucia Range mountain slopes and broad alluvial terraces; 700-1,800 ft.

SOIL:

Broad alluvial terraces and fans of Paso Robles Creek and the Salinas River over bedrock; alluvial soils of shallow to moderate depth and sandy to silty to clay loams; calcareous in places.

DIURNAL SWING: 20-40°F
ANNUAL PRECIPITATION: 20"
WINKLER INDEX: II

The story of the Templeton Gap District is well rooted in viticulture. It is one of the oldest planted regions in California and only recently received its current name, thanks to the wine industry. Grape growing in the region began in 1856, when Adolph Siot planted the first vineyard along a road now known as Vineyard Drive.

▼

(For more on Siot see page 49.) He established a commercial winery adjacent to the vineyard in 1890 and was the only local commercial winemaker until 1917.

The Rotta family purchased Siot's vineyard and winery in 1908 and renamed it Rotta Winery. Nearby, the Pesenti family planted grapes in 1923 and established their namesake winery in 1934. Both wineries gained local reputations for fine, affordable zinfandels.

In 1924, Sylvester Dusi planted zinfandel at Dusi Ranch, located three miles south of Paso Robles and east of Highway 101.

The Dusi family farmed and sold zinfandel grapes for more than 80 years, finally establishing a permanent winery three generations later.

An expansion of grape growing and winemaking in the region began in 1976, when Pasquale Mastan started Mastantuono Winery near the corner of Highway 46 West and Vineyard Road.

▼

Ken Volk established a vineyard and eventually a winery along Templeton Road southeast of Templeton in 1982, calling it Wild Horse Winery and Vineyard. Fratelli Perata was established in 1989, only the twelfth commercial winery in the six-year-old Paso Robles AVA at that point. Hope Family Wines/Austin Hope Winery, then called Hope Farms Winery, was established in 1990 on Highway 46. Expansion would continue along this stretch of highway within the Templeton Gap District as it was seen as prime land not only for growing grapes, but for the eventual tourism trade. Visitors can access several wineries strung along this busy thoroughfare.

The name Templeton Gap is of recent origin, and it's a term that originated in the wine industry. It is widely accepted that Ken Volk coined "Templeton Gap" in 1982 when he began planting a vineyard east of the town.

He used it to describe the route by which cool afternoon winds flowed inland from the Pacific Ocean through passes in the Santa Lucia Range, especially during the summer and early fall.

Volk noted that the breeze helped to moderate temperatures in the vineyards around the Templeton area, including his own, as well as areas south and west of Paso Robles. To break it down further, the name combines "Templeton," the nearby town founded in 1886, and "gap," in the sense of its landform definition: "a geological formation that is a low point or opening between hills or mountains or in a ridge or mountain range."

The first time Templeton Gap appeared in writing was on Wild Horse Winery and Vineyards' marketing and public relations material. Eventually, references to the Templeton Gap would appear in *The Wine Atlas of California and the Pacific Northwest* by Bob Thompson in 1993, in a Sunset Magazine article titled "California's Heritage Wine" by Lora J. Finnegan in 1995, as well as *The Wines of California* by Stephen Brook in 1999.

The Pacific Ocean is approximately 18 nautical miles to the city of Paso Robles from its closest point at the town of Cayucos, which sits at the inner apex of Estero Bay. The western border of the Templeton Gap District is much closer to that point, and as the marine layer builds across Estero Bay to altitudes of 1,400–1,800 feet the heavier air spills across the range crest, easily seen on some days as large fingers of fog reaching over the mountains like a massive fog monster.

▼

This cool air spills through the gap along the Highway 46 West corridor and continues to flow to the lower elevations to the east, across the Templeton Gap viticultural area, and into the El Pomar District, Creston District, and the Paso Robles Estrella District. The warm days of Paso Robles have a direct cause and effect on this cooling influence. As the temperature gradient rises a vacuum effect pulls the spilling cool air inland and, like clockwork, by 3 p.m. the cool breeze begins.

Although cooling winds can find their way inland up and down the coastal range, it is the aligning of factors that create the very specific Templeton Gap effect that helps to not only cool off the Templeton Gap District, but many other parts of the greater Paso Robles AVA. There is a slight overall topographic elevation drop that aligns with Estero Bay, as well as east-to-west ravines that are conducive to channeling airflow. Although Estero Bay does not have a submarine canyon, the water remains cold year-round, adding to the climatic uniqueness of the region through advection fog, which is the combination of a cool surface mixing with warm moist air.

▼

Because of this accelerated air flow through the gap, the Templeton Gap District is windier than much of the rest of the Paso Robles AVA. It also sits up against the coastal mountains and extends to the east with lower elevations, well within the rain shadow of the mountains. This results in an average of 20 inches of rain per year.

Many of the vineyards are planted on south-facing slopes, directly receiving the maritime air as it flows from the gap. The cool climate increases the ripening period for grapes, resulting in longer hangtime with harvest dates as much as two weeks later than nearby AVAs. This area is conducive to wine grape varieties that excel in cool climates, including pinot noir and chardonnay. The natural vegetation reflects the climate of the region as well, with mixed woodlands over most of the area, transitioning to more open oak woodlands at the lowest elevations where it is slightly drier.

The Templeton Gap District is considered one of the coolest of the Paso Robles AVAs. It is a Type II region according to the Winkler scale, which gives it an average 2,900 growing degree days. This is equivalent to Old World growing regions such as the Duoro Valley, Piedmont and Bordeaux, all of them also in the 2,900 range.

▼

The geology of the Templeton Gap District is essentially a result of uplift from the Santa Lucia Range west of the Rinconada fault as well as considerable erosion of the soft Monterey formation marine shales, mudstones, siltstones and sandstones.

The eastern slope of the Santa Lucia Range rises dramatically from the Salinas River, forming the western and northern boundaries of the district.

As you travel east, you'll encounter channels and floodplains created by the Salinas River and various creeks, resulting in the exposure of higher alluvial terraces and fans. Sloped hills and cuestas frame the district to the south.

Soils are mostly the Linne-Calodo complex of alkaline clay loams on hillsides and river terraces. On the steepest slopes you will find the Gaviota-rock gravelly loam, and most terraces consist of the Lockwood-Concepion complex of shaly loams. Although some places have slightly acidic top soils with pH values of 6.1 to 6.8, others are neutral to slightly alkaline even at the surface with pH values of 7.0 to 7.8.

▼

The terroir of the Templeton Gap District possesses some ideal conditions for the cultivation of excellent wine grapes, with shallow to moderate soil rooting depths, moderate water stress, modest nutrient levels, and the cool climate and long growing season that allows a diverse array of wine grapes to flourish.

It's no wonder why this area was identified long ago as a prime place to grow some of the first commercially available wine grapes and wines in not just Paso Robles, but California.

TODAY THERE ARE APPROXIMATELY 20 WINERIES WITHIN THE TEMPLETON GAP DISTRICT'S 35,000 ACRES.

▼

SOUTHWEST

SANTA MARGARITA RANCH

Ancient Peaks Winery

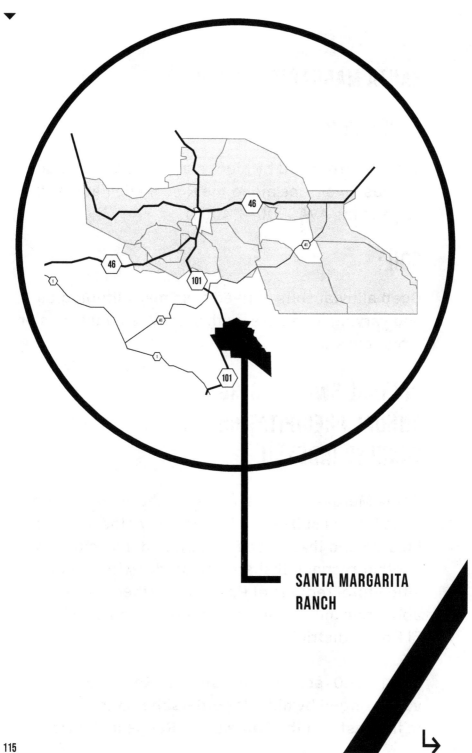

**SANTA MARGARITA
RANCH**

SANTA MARGARITA RANCH

TOPOGRAPHY:

Valley surrounded by high, steep mountain slopes. Salinas River runs along the Rinconada Fault at the edge of the AVA. 900–1,400 ft.

SOIL:

Deep alluvial soils derived from many lithologies and varying in texture, with patchy residual soils on mountain slopes.

DIURNAL SWING: 20-30°F
ANNUAL PRECIPITATION: 29"
WINKLER INDEX: II

Santa Margarita Ranch is the southernmost of the Paso Robles sub-AVAs (it's actually closer to San Luis Obispo than Paso Robles), and it's unique in another respect: it shares no border with any other viticultural regions of Paso. Its northern border lies about five miles south of the Templeton Gap and El Pomar districts.

The 18,300-acre Santa Margarita Ranch AVA is a valley ringed by hills. It borders the Salinas River in the east and the Santa Lucia Range in the west.

▼

In the southwest, it abuts the Los Padres National Forest. The northern border winds its way from the Salinas River, following Santa Margarita Road in Atascadero to its western edge.

This AVA is mostly 900 to 1,400 feet above sea level, but there are few vineyards above the valley floor; those plantings lie at 1,000 to 1,225 feet. Although the Templeton Gap is too far north to play a factor in the area's climate, maritime air and some coastal fog influence the valley by way of Cuesta Pass, but its effects are not dramatic. Rainfall compares to other wetter spots on the west side, averaging just under 30 inches per year. Its southerly location in relation to the rest of the greater Paso Robles AVA gives Rancho Santa Margarita warmer days and a longer growing season, although occasional frosts can present a challenge. It is considered a Region II climate zone.

The Santa Margarita Ranch AVA has very diverse bedrock and soil types that set it apart from the other Paso Robles AVAs. It's a visually stunning place, with oak savanna on the valley floor and chaparral and mixed woodlands on the hillslopes, and many creeks and streams that cut the landscape.

▼

It's no wonder it was identified by settlers as a place to establish an early agricultural and commercial hub.

The headwaters of the Salinas River begin in the surrounding mountains and feed the river from the spillway of Santa Margarita Lake. Historically this region was seen as a lush oasis, perfect for farming a multitude of crops and for grazing land.

The name Santa Margarita originates with the original Mexican land grant in the mid-1800s, which was itself named after the unique mission that existed there, the Santa Margarita de Cortona Asistencia.

By definition, an asistencia was "a mission on a small scale with all the requisites for a mission, and with Divine Service held regularly on days of obligation, except that it lacked a resident priest."

At the time that the Asistencia was built, grapevines were planted on the ranch by the Franciscan friars. Much like the rest of California during the establishment of the mission system, farming and the raising of livestock was introduced, which caused profound changes in the lives of the native population.

▼

IN THE DECADES FOLLOWING
THE END OF THE MISSION ERA,
SANTA MARGARITA WOULD BECOME
A WELLS FARGO STAGECOACH WAY
STATION AS WELL AS A TRAIN
STOP FOR THE SOUTHERN
PACIFIC RAILROAD.

▼

AFTER THE MISSION ERA, VITICULTURE PLAYED NO MAJOR ROLE IN THE REGION'S AGRICULTURAL DEVELOPMENT UNTIL ROBERT MONDAVI WINERY LEASED OVER 1,000 ACRES FOR VINEYARD DEVELOPMENT IN THE 2000s.

Many years of planting and development ensued, as well as a change of ownership. The vineyard developed by Mondavi Winery is now over 850 acres with 16 varieties of wine grapes.

A distinctive maritime and mountain-valley climate exists in Santa Margarita Ranch. Regions to the north, like the Templeton Gap and Paso Robles Willow Creek districts, have lower daytime highs and slightly higher nighttime lows due to the influence of the Templeton Gap.

The narrow valley of the Santa Margarita Ranch is surrounded by mountains on three sides so the maritime influence is less pervasive, and there are orographic influences that bring more rainfall.

▼

The Santa Margarita Ranch viticultural area is nestled up against the Santa Lucia Range and contains the familiar marine sedimentary material that can be found throughout the Paso Robles region. However, Santa Margarita also has granitic rock, the result of faulting and movement along the San Andreas fault zone over the last few million years, which accompanied the uplift of the Santa Lucia Range.

The valley floor of the Santa Margarita area was originally formed by erosion from the Salinas River. At some point the river carved a channel through the soft Monterey Formation shales along the Rinconada Fault as the San Andreas Fault zone became more active. This created a broad alluvial fan and terrace deposits across the area, largely at the 1,150-1,350-foot elevation. The viticultural landscape also contains deep, gravelly loam soils as well as shallower clay loam soils against the bedrock on hillsides. Sandy loam soils in the floodplains of the creeks are abundant within the valley.

A curiosity of the region is its large, fossilized oyster shells, which are as abundant as stars in the sky. This is reflective of an ancient shallow seabed that allowed oysters to thrive, growing into exceptionally large specimens.

▼

SOUTHEAST

EL POMAR DISTRICT

DENO Wines
Hidden Oak Winery
Rava Wines
Still Waters Vineyards
The Fabelist

EL POMAR DISTRICT

▼

EL POMAR DISTRICT

TOPOGRAPHY:

Higher, older terraces, fans and hills. 740-1,600 ft.

SOIL:

Alluvial soils, well-developed loams to clay loams, some calcareous, with Monterey Formation sandstone and siltstone at depth in some areas.

DIURNAL SWING: 20-35°F
ANNUAL PRECITITATION: 15"
WINKLER INDEX: II

At the center of the greater Paso Robles AVA is the El Pomar District. Like much of California's central coast, agriculture has everything to do with its name. Derived from the Latin word pomum, or edible fruit, it has commonly come to mean orchard in Spanish. Nut orchards, mostly almonds, were long the primary fruit in the El Pomar District.

Many orchards were planted as early as 1886, and by 1968 El Pomar had 1,375 acres of almonds and 36 acres of walnuts.

▼

At its height, many considered the El Pomar region the almond capital of California, with rumors that Hershey was looking to develop a plant in the area.

Over time the almond industry moved to the San Joaquin Valley, where flatter land and better access to water proved more efficient than dry farming on hillsides. Today, many of those orchards are being replaced by vineyards as the Paso Robles wine industry continues to grow.

The El Pomar District encompasses approximately 21,300 acres, with a little over 2,000 acres under vine. Vineyards in the region are not new; they have been recorded as early as the late 1800s. In 1886, Gerd Klintworth planted a vineyard on a property that is now named Red Head Ranch, near Cripple Creek Road at the eastern edge of the district.

The El Pomar landscape comprises old river terraces and escarpments, alluvial fans, and dry creek beds sitting at the base of the foothills of the La Panza Range. East of the Rinconada Fault, the Santa Lucia Range and the Salinas River, El Pomar lies in an area of uplift along the La Panza and Huero faults.

▼

Elevations here range from about 740 feet near the Salinas River and Paso Robles city limits to 1,600 feet on ridge tops.

MOST VINEYARDS ARE AT ELEVATIONS OF 840 FEET TO 960 FEET, BUT A FEW ARE PLANTED ON HIGHER HILLS AROUND 1,440 FEET.

Many vineyards are situated on rolling land. The area experiences different sources of air movement that influence climate, primarily the Templeton Gap effect.

In the summer and fall, the marine layer builds to a greater height in Estero Bay, approximately 15 nautical miles from the center of the El Pomar District.

Once that layer reaches altitudes of 1,400–1,800 feet, the heavier marine air flows over the lower ridges of the Santa Lucia Range, spilling through the Templeton Gap, which follows State Route 46.

▼

Data collected from a vineyard near the junction of El Pomar Drive and South El Pomar Road show daily maximum winds of 10-20 miles per hour during the growing season, reflecting the sea breeze through the Templeton Gap. The El Pomar District can have a diurnal temperature swing of 20-35F during these warmer months.

El Pomar's climate is ideal for several Bordeaux varieties, including merlot, cabernet sauvignon and cabernet franc. It's also suitable for Rhône varieties.

As is the case for the entire region, rainfall decreases the further east one travels from the Santa Lucia Range. It drops from about 20 inches annually in the Templeton Gap District to 15 inches in the El Pomar District and 11.5 inches in the Creston District just to the east of El Pomar.

The geology of El Pomar mirrors many portions of the districts west of the Salinas River. Late Cretaceous granitic plutons (massive, ancient formations) are its basement, as well as late Cretaceous marine sedimentary rocks (mostly sandstones) to the south.

▼

Many of these soils have calcareous shale fragments, with secondary lime deposited as wind and rain help to erode and move soil over time.

These moderate alkaline soils are excellent for growing wine grapes and can impart great natural acidity to the wines.

The El Pomar District has almost ideal conditions for premium wine grapes, with shallow to moderate soil rooting depths, moderate water stress, modest nutrient levels and a cool climate, leading to the development of complex fruit flavors.

As evidenced by the orchards planted in the area between the late 1880s and the 1920s, these distinctive growing conditions have been appreciated by farmers for a very long time.

Orchards are returning to El Pomar, with many ranchers planting olive groves to produce artisanal olive oil. As more trees are planted, the region is being transformed into landscapes of bucolic agrarian beauty that are reminiscent of Europe at times.

▼

▼

SOUTHEAST

CRESTON DISTRICT

Aleksander Wines
B&E Vineyard and Winery
Chateau Margene
Saxby Winery And Vineyard
Shadow Run Vineyards

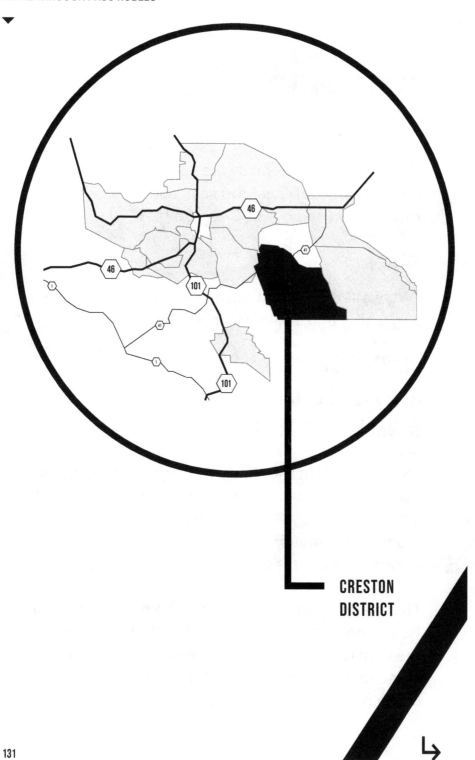

**CRESTON
DISTRICT**

CRESTON DISTRICT

TOPOGRAPHY:

Old erosional plateau at the base of the La Panza Range; alluvial terraces and fans of Huerhuero Creek; 1,000–2,000 ft.

SOIL:

Old, well-developed terrace and hillside soils; mix of granitic and sedimentary rocks.

DIURNAL SWING: 25-35°F
ANNUAL PRECIPITATION: 11.5"
WINKLER INDEX: III

The Creston District has a rich agricultural history that stretches back to the late 1800s and remains influential today. This region is largely lomas montuosas (mountainous hills), a stretch of rolling land covered with trees.

This made it perfect for cattle and horse ranching. As you head southeast from Paso Robles and enter the Creston District it looks much the same as it did in the last decades of the 19th century, with many cattle ranches still thriving.

Today, vineyards complement the bucolic landscape with a beauty that can easily be described as Old California.

Although it was first called Huerhuero in the original land grant of 1842, the town's present name of Creston was adopted in 1885; later the name was used to describe the area surrounding it as the Creston District.

Around this time, the first grapes were planted in the Creston District. One of the founding fathers, J.V. Webster, an experienced horticulturist, showcased his grapes at the 1888 county fair.

Mirroring the greater Paso Robles AVA's early growth as a wine region, Creston was recognized even in the late 1800s as a wine region of potential.

The Creston District has areas of medium to high elevation, ranging from 1,000 to 2,000 feet, encompassing old river terraces as well as mountain foothills.

▼

Situated at the base of the La Panza Range, this area has been subject to uplift from the La Panza Fault (as well as the adjacent Huerhuero Fault), which has allowed creeks to erode the land and reveal granitic rocks, sandstone, and the Monterey formation shale that is so prevalent throughout the Paso Robles AVA.

Creston's geographic position on the map of the Paso Robles AVA plays another key role in its identity. As one travels southeast from the city of Paso Robles, leaving the Santa Lucia Range and Salinas River to the northwest, the land transforms quickly to rolling savanna.

Looking back to the west, the outline of the Santa Lucia Range appears taller to the north, with a noticeable dip in the ridge line almost parallel to Creston. This is the Templeton Gap.

The Creston District has an average diurnal temperature swing of 25°-35°F and occasionally sees swings as high as 50°F.

Huerhuero Creek is the major watershed of the Creston District. This creek bisects the region and is dry most of the year, exposing a sandy bed, typical of the soil found in the lower elevations of the district.

▼

Hillsides and higher elevations give way to clay loams on the terraces. During exceptionally wet years, the Huerhuero, a major tributary of the Salinas River, winds its way northwest, causing considerable erosion.

The District is within the rain shadow of the Santa Lucia Range, with precipitation decreasing from about 20 inches in the Templeton Gap District, to 15 inches in the El Pomar District, to 11.5 inches in Creston. It takes far more than 11.5 inches in a year for the Huerhuero to flow vigorously.

The Creston District is approximately 47,000 acres, with more than 1,400 under vine.

Vineyards are mostly planted at elevations of 1,000 to 1,300 feet, with some found higher — up to 1,800 feet. Many are on west- and southwest-facing slopes, absorbing the breezes ushered in through the Templeton Gap.

The Creston District has been notably friendly to Bordeaux varieties, especially cabernet sauvignon. As a Winkler III district, Rhône varieties can be grown here as well.

Of course, the vineyard manager knows his land the best, so depending on aspect, soil, elevation, and all the things that make the Creston District unique, many things are possible.

Wine tasting in the Creston District feels a little like stepping back in time. Wide-open spaces surround most wineries, and the region's narrow roads rise and fall from grassy hillsides down to dry creek beds. Much like the ranches and homesteads of Creston, wineries, vineyards, and tasting rooms are spread out across the district, each showcasing the pioneering spirit of Creston in their architecture and landscaping. It's an attractive and historic district that embodies the soul of the greater Paso Robles AVA.

▼

▼

SOUTHEAST

PASO ROBLES HIGHLANDS DISTRICT

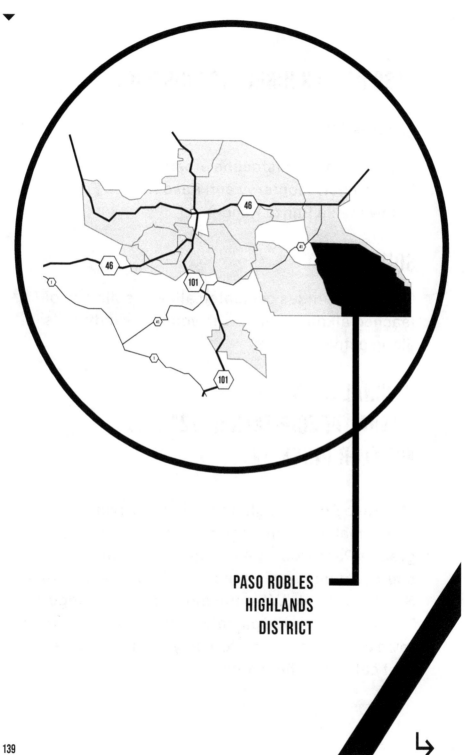

**PASO ROBLES
HIGHLANDS
DISTRICT**

▼

PASO ROBLES HIGHLANDS DISTRICT

TOPOGRAPHY:

Old Pliocene-Pleistocene erosional surface across the Simmler, Monterey and Paso Robles Formations below the La Panza Range.

SOIL:

Deep, sometimes cemented alluvial soils and old leached alkaline soils, with younger sandy soils along active streams.

DIURNAL SWING: 30-50°F
ANNUAL PRECIPITATION: 12"
WINKLER INDEX: IV

The Paso Robles Highlands District covers 60,300 acres, making it the second largest within the greater Paso Robles AVA. This region fills in the southeast quadrant of the Paso Robles AVA with the San Juan Creek AVA outlining its northern edge. The area has been sparsely settled, with no formal town or settlement; historically it was known as a vast cattle ranching area.

Residents of this region have used the name "Highlands" since at least the late 1800s.

The Highlands School District, located largely within the proposed viticultural area, appears in local records as early as 1890.

Cattle ranching was the main business in the Highlands for many years. In the early 1900s, well-known businessman Bernard Sinsheimer and other family members were major landowners and established a working cattle ranch in the region. Descendants of Sinsheimer continue to operate a large cattle ranch within the Highlands District.

Viticulture in the Highlands District began in the 1970s with three major vineyards that are still around today: Shell Creek Vineyard, Shandon Hills Vineyard and French Camp Vineyards.

Shell Creek Vineyard gets its name from a creek that runs through the property and in wet years can be seen carrying small pieces of fossilized shells that can be found further upstream.

Shell Creek Vineyard was planted in 1972. It does not have a brand associated with it but is known as a source vineyard for exceptional petite sirah and syrah, as well as cabernet sauvignon, chenin blanc and valdigue.

Shandon Hills Vineyard was also planted in 1972 and was originally a part of Shell Creek Vineyard. The Sinton family, who are descendants of the Sinsheimers, planted both vineyards and continue to own the latter. Much like Shell Creek Vineyard, Shandon Hills Vineyard is not associated with any brand but serves as a source for multiple wineries throughout the Paso Robles AVA. Planted to petite sirah, zinfandel, chardonnay, cabernet sauvignon and sauvignon blanc, this vast planting sits on 165 acres.

French Camp Vineyards is the largest single vineyard in the Paso Robles AVA. It is named after a site where two French sheepherders were notoriously murdered in 1857. This vast parcel consists of 5,600 acres of land that is owned by the Miller Family, who also owns multiple wine brands including J. Wilkes Wines, Ballard Lane, Barrel Burner, and Smashberry, which showcases French Camp fruit.

However, a majority of the wine grapes grown at French Camp are sold to wineries in Paso Robles, which designate the vineyard on their labels. The vineyard began to be planted in 1973 and today there are a bit less than 2,000 total acres under vine. More than 20 different varieties are grown here, both white and red.

The Highlands District has the highest consistent elevation of all the AVAs in Paso Robles, with a range of 1,160-2,086 feet (most vineyards are at 1,200-1,600 feet). At 33 miles from the Pacific Ocean, this AVA generally has a warmer and more continental climate with less precipitation than other regions of the Paso Robles viticultural area at similar elevations.

Due to its location to the east of the Santa Lucia Range and northeast of the La Panza Range, the Highlands District lies in a double rain shadow.

However, due to its relatively higher elevations, it still receives an average of 12 inches of precipitation annually, which is a little more than some of the other Paso Robles AVAs to the north and west.

The Highlands District experiences the greatest day-to-night temperature change in the entire Paso Robles AVA, and it has greater daily, monthly, seasonal and annual temperature ranges than other regions within the overall viticultural area.

The difference between daily maximum and minimum temperatures in the mid and late summer can be 50F or more, with highs around 100 and lows around 50.

ACCORDING TO GRAPE GROWERS IN THE REGION, THE WARM SUMMER DAYS ENSURE THE FULL MATURITY OF THE FRUIT, WHILE THE COOL EVENINGS PRESERVE ACIDS IN THE GRAPES.

The growers also note that due to its distinctive climate, grape harvest occurs two to four weeks earlier than most other regions of the Paso Robles viticultural area.

The soil in the Highlands District is predominantly sandy loam along the creeks, loams on the small alluvial fans, and coarse sandy loams to clay loams on the hillsides. Many of the subsoils are cemented by calcium carbonate, which can cause vines to struggle for the first five to 10 years until they reach deeper to find iron-based clay.

This increases vigor in the vines and produces intensely rich fruit.

The Paso Robles Highlands District can be visually stunning — locals know that its vast plains are the perfect place to view wildflowers in the spring.

It's an unsung region that is well removed from the rest of the Paso Robles AVA, yet it provides the secret ingredient in many wineries' best offerings.

From aglianico to chenin blanc, its intense varieties are blended into a wide array of excellent Paso wines.

▼

SOUTHEAST
SAN JUAN CREEK

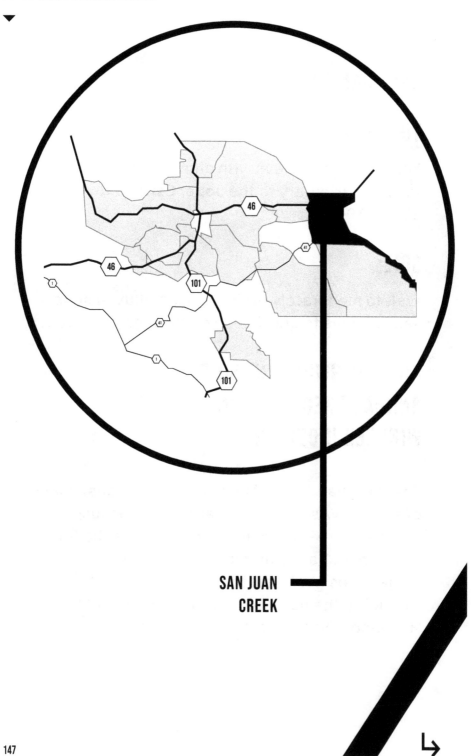

SAN JUAN
CREEK

▼

SAN JUAN CREEK

TOPOGRAPHY:

Younger river valleys with alluvial terraces and fans as a tributary to the upper Estrella River; 980-1,600 ft.

SOIL:

Well to moderately drained, deep alluvial soils, sandy loams to clay loams on the highest terraces.

DIURNAL SWING: 35-50°F
ANNUAL PRECIPITATION: 10.4"
WINKLER INDEX: III

The San Juan Creek AVA may be the oddest shaped of the 11 AVAs in Paso, in large part because a southeastern-stretching finger follows the San Juan Creek Valley that interacts with the easternmost AVAs as it touches the Estrella District to the north of San Juan Creek and the Highlands District to its south.

▼

San Juan Creek was named after Saint John, which was a popular place name in old pre-statehood California. As one of the earliest land grants in San Luis Obispo County, it was named San Juan Capistrano del Camate. This area amounted to about 30 square miles of land, but in 1846 the grant was deemed legally unallowable by the United States government. It eventually was parceled out and purchased by individuals. Early historical accounts named this creek both San Juan Creek and the Estrella River, but today it is well established that San Juan Creek is a tributary that comes together with Cholame Creek to form the Estrella River.

At the confluence of the two creeks is the town of Shandon. Once named Starkey, it changed its name to Cholame in the late 1880s. Shandon's population was sparse in the late 19th century and remains well below 2,000 today. The San Juan Creek area has long been a ranching, vineyard, and field-and-row crop farming community. At one point the area attracted a fledgling farmer, Walter Knott, who grew produce for the ranch hands in the area and sold what was not consumed. By 1920, Knott moved to Southern California to begin a berry farm which eventually became one of the region's great roadside attractions, Knott's Berry Farm.

▼

It was not until the 1960s that commercial grape farming found its way to San Juan Creek. In 1963, Robert Young planted a vineyard in Shandon. Mr. Young is known as the first new commercial grape grower in the region after the end of Prohibition, as well as the first to incorporate a commercial irrigation system in Paso Robles. In 1971, Darryl John moved to Shandon and planted the San Juan Vineyard for Louie Lucas of Lucas & Lewellen. Early varieties included zinfandel, carignan, cabernet sauvignon, sauvignon blanc, muscat and chenin blanc.

The San Juan Creek AVA consists of about 26,000 acres, with a little over 3,000 acres under vine. Elevations in the district range from 980 feet to 1,600 feet, encompassing both river valleys and foothills. The landscape of the district is influenced by the San Andreas Fault and adjacent San Juan Fault, which create significant uplift and subsequent erosion of the mountain ranges. This provides for some stunning land formations that are very photogenic. San Juan Creek follows the path of the San Juan Fault, a shallow fault system which has visibly fractured the earth.

▼

The broad alluvial plain of the AVA consists of mostly loamy sands, gravelly to sandy clay loams, and a few clays on the older alluvial fans and terraces. These create moderate draining conditions in the vineyards which encourage vigor in the vines. It also provides an environment for deep soil-rooting and some moderate to high water stress. With the abundance of sunshine in the San Juan Creek AVA, moderate yields are harvested at earlier dates than in the cooler regions to the west.

The San Juan Creek AVA is about 32 miles from the Pacific Ocean and within the rain shadow of the Santa Lucia Range, so it has a warmer and more continental climate than some of the other Paso Robles AVAs to the west.

There is a descending air movement that takes place in the rainy season down the lee slopes of the coastal range, as well as the La Panza Range to the south. As a result, rainfall decreases from about 20 inches annually in the Templeton Gap District to around 10 inches in the San Juan Creek AVA. That's a 50 percent reduction in rainfall in less than 20 miles.

▼

San Juan Creek can get exceptionally warm during the summer as it is a Region III – IV on the Winkler Scale, although the nights still get quite cool, with an average diurnal temperature swing of 35-40 F.

THIS GROWING DEGREE CLIMATE IS SUITED TO SEVERAL BORDEAUX VARIETIES, INCLUDING CABERNET SAUVIGNON, MERLOT AND CABERNET FRANC.

However, many growers are seeing success with petite sirah and some Italian and Spanish varieties as well.

There are no winery brands associated with the San Juan Creek AVA; however, the vineyards located there are a primary source of grapes for a multitude of wineries throughout the Paso Robles wine region.

▼

NORTHEAST

PASO ROBLES GENESEO DISRICT

Barr Estate Winery
Cass Winery
Eberle Winery
Gelfand Vineyards
Glunz Family Winery & Cellars
Pear Valley Estate Wine
Penman Springs Vineyard
Sculpterra Winery
Steinbeck Vineyards & Winery
Tobin James Cellars
Vina Robles Vineyards & Winery

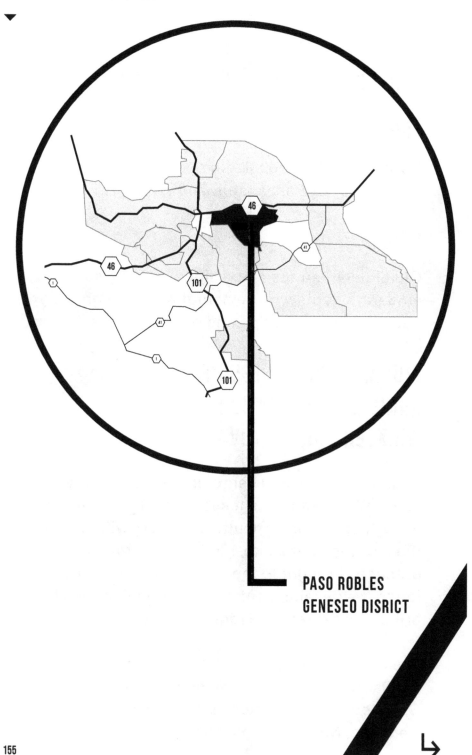

**PASO ROBLES
GENESEO DISRICT**

▼

GENESEO DISTRICT

TOPOGRAPHY:

Upfaulted hills through old river terraces along Huerhuero-La Panza fault. 740-1,300 ft.

SOIL:

Old alluvial terrace and residual hillside soils of moderate depth with cementation of the gravelly Paso Robles Formation and older granites.

DIURNAL SWING: 30-50°F
ANNUAL PRECIPITATION: 13-14"
WINKLER INDEX: III-IV

Positioned front and center in the Paso Robles AVA is the 17,300-acre Geneseo District. This region has a fascinating agricultural history with links to the Midwest in the late 1800s. The farming practices brought to the region by early settlers led to the development of exceptional grapes that brilliantly express the region's terroir.

The Geneseo District, christened as such in the 1880s, took its name from the small town of Geneseo, Illinois, which in turn was named for Geneseo, New York.

▼

"Geneseo" is an Iroquois word that roughly translates as shining or beautiful valley. As the story goes, the first settlers arriving in the lands near the Heurhuero River sent an advertisement to the Geneseo Republic newspaper in Illinois, encouraging people to come west because there was an abundance of optimal farmland in the area.

One of those families, the Ernsts, saw a great opportunity and made the 2,000-mile trek to California, bringing along their farming traditions.

Located approximately 11 miles east of Paso Robles, Geneseo was established with a one-room schoolhouse. The Midwesterners also brought along their faith, establishing the first Lutheran Church in the area; services were held in both German and English. During these times it was common for pioneer communities to be made up of many different European cultures. There was a small Swedish settlement a little northwest of Geneseo.

Farming and ranching in the region began with grain crops, garden produce, fruit and nut orchards, as well as cattle and horses.

▼

In 1884, the Ernst family planted the first vineyards, consisting of more than 20 varieties of wine grapes. The descendants of the Ernst family (Steinbeck Vineyards & Winery) continue to farm in the Geneseo District. Now in their seventh generation, the Ernsts continue to celebrate family, faith and stewardship while sharing their love for the region.

The Geneseo District is largely made up of a series of terraces surrounding the Estrella River and Huerhuero Creek.

Much like stair steps, these terraces rise and fall across the region, which gives growers many options regarding aspect. They can plant on southwest, southeast, northwest, and northeast exposures as they see fit.

A relatively warm region, Geneseo benefits from the cooling influences of the Templeton Gap effect, which fluctuates day to night temperatures by up to 50F, providing a prime opportunity for grape clusters to ripen yet cool off overnight.

▼

This influences sugar production during the day and allows the skins and acid to develop in the evening, ultimately leading to wines that deftly balance alcohol, tannin and acid.

The soils in the Geneseo District are mostly silty clay and clay loam, with some decomposed calcareous material well below the surface.

These soils range from more acidic in the clay material (5.6 – 6.5 pH) to more alkaline in the calcareous zones (7.9 – 8.4 pH). This can influence vigor, depending on how densely impacted the soil is, but moderate soil rooting depths, moderate water stress and modest to low nutrient levels are the norm.

Stressed-out vines can develop some very complex fruit flavors, so winemakers have opted to grow many of the Bordeaux varieties in this region, along with some Rhône varieties such as syrah, which is represented by some of the oldest such vineyards in all of Paso Robles.

▼

Although wine grapes were planted in the late 1800s within the Geneseo District, it was not until the 1970s that some larger-scale plantings took place. Quality winemaking really took off in the 1980s. The Steinbecks, along with Gary Eberle, established many of those first commercial vineyards, followed by the Arciero Family (formerly EOS Winery) and the Bianchi Family, and many more brands followed. In 2005, Cass Vineyard was established in the southeast corner of the Geneseo District with 145 acres under vine.

New plantings have slowed in the region, principally because of the limited water supply within the aquifer, but the Geneseo District continues to mature. Wines from the district are known for pronounced aromas and flavors, and Geneseo fruit is often sourced by brands from all over the Paso Robles AVA.

▼

▼

NORTHEAST

PASO ROBLES ESTRELLA DISTRICT

Allegretto Wines
Bodega de Edgar
Broken Earth Winery
Graveyard Vineyards
Hearst Ranch Winery
J. Lohr Vineyards & Wines
Le Vigne Winery
RN Estate Vineyard and Winery
Sea Shell Cellars

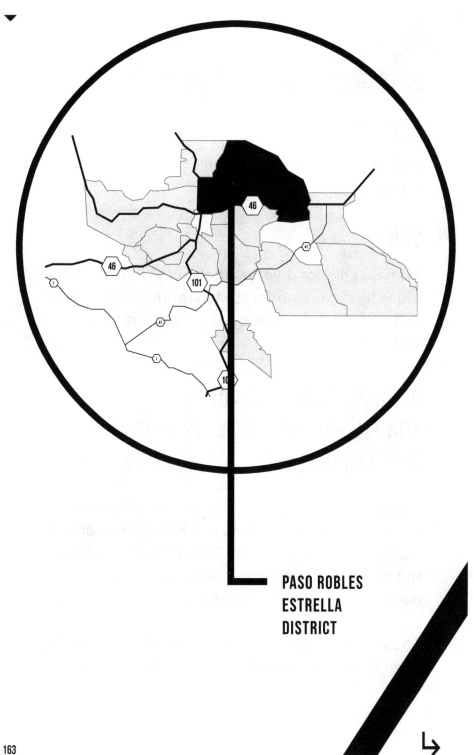

**PASO ROBLES
ESTRELLA
DISTRICT**

▼

PASO ROBLES ESTRELLA DISTRICT

TOPOGRAPHY:

Rolling plains of Estrella River Valley and terraces. 745-1,800 ft.

SOIL:

Alluvial soils of diverse ages across younger to older terraces, moderate to significant in depth, with remnant patches of older soils at highest elevations.

DIURNAL SWING: 35-40F
ANNUAL PRECIPITATION: 12.5-15.5"
WINKLER INDEX: III

When the Spanish and Mexican governments created large land grants in what is now coastal California from the late 1700s to the mid-1800s, the settlers of the period were responsible for the naming of rivers, mountains and large areas of land.

Those place names remained, for the most part, after California became the 31st state in 1850.

▼

The Estrella District was first noted by that name shortly after statehood as the region was starting to become homesteaded. It is within the area bounded by the La Estrella Mexican land grant of 1844. Estrella, or "star" in Spanish, gains its name because of the interesting pattern made by some ridge lines that seemingly come together like the rays of a star at the convergence of four valleys. The river that runs through the area also received the name Estrella.

As farmers and homesteaders moved to the region, the town of Estrella was founded in 1886. Oddly enough, one of the town's founders, a man by the name of Gordanier, stipulated that "no vinous beverages nor spirituous malt or other intoxicating liquid shall be manufactured, sold, or kept for sale on the Gordanier side of town." Little did he know that the future of this region lay in the growth and production of exceptional grapes that would be transformed into world-class wines.

Agriculture in the Estrella District was challenging until the railroad came to San Miguel shortly before Paso Robles' incorporation as a city in 1889. Dry-farmed grain and feed, cattle and sheep were the main sources of livelihood in the region.

▼

It was a testament to their resilience, but not until the arrival of the railroad could these farmers and ranchers get their product reliably to market in Los Angeles or San Francisco. The coming of the railroad allowed more people to establish roots in the area.

The district's importance to viticulture is rooted in a syrah clone called the Estrella Clone. It was named after the Estrella River Winery, which planted syrah in 1975 using cuttings from the Chapoutier vineyard in France's celebrated northern Rhône AOC, Hermitage. The idea to plant the first commercial syrah vineyard in California was the inspiration of Paso wine pioneer Gary Eberle, founding winemaker at the Estrella River Winery and current owner of Eberle Winery.

Covering approximately 66,800 acres in the floodplain of the Estrella River, the Estrella District has a typical valley floor-type topography. The Estrella River, mostly a dry riverbed, forms near the town of Shandon and flows west-northwest to the Salinas River. Its headwaters emanate from the confluence of Cholame Creek and San Juan Creek, which are fed by waters flowing down the mountain from the Temblor and La Panza ranges.

Elevations in the Estrella District range between 745 and 1,800 feet through a series of terraces and foothills. Vineyards are planted on flat plains and various slope angles and aspects. The warm summer days are cooled by modest maritime sea breezes through the Templeton Gap, as well as downslope winds from the eastern ranges, marked by early morning fog in the summer.

The soils in the Estrella are predominantly alluvial in nature, ranging from fine sandy loams to more substantial clay loam. The terroir is perfect for the cultivation of premium wine grapes: warm days that lead to cool nights, moderate soil rooting depths that control vigor in the vines, and tempered water stress to produce complex fruit flavors. Besides syrah, red varieties that do well in the Estrella District include cabernet sauvignon, merlot, petite sirah, and other Bordeaux grapes. White varieties that thrive here include sauvignon blanc, viognier and chardonnay.

The late 1960s and early '70s saw an influx of next-generation vineyard pioneers who had come to focus on the Paso Robles region, specifically the Estrella area.

▼

Brands like J. Lohr Vineyards & Wines, Estrella River Winery (which eventually became Meridian Vineyards), and Continental Vineyards (now Broken Earth Winery) had the vision to plant in the Estrella. Bringing university training and financial resources, these winemakers were able to develop large swaths of land and learn over time which varieties were best suited to the terroir. Much like the original homesteaders, they took a leap of faith that has led to great success.

▼

▼

NORTHEAST

SAN MIGUEL DISTRICT

Locatelli Vineyards & Winery
Mystic Hills Vineyard
Vista Del Rey Vineyards

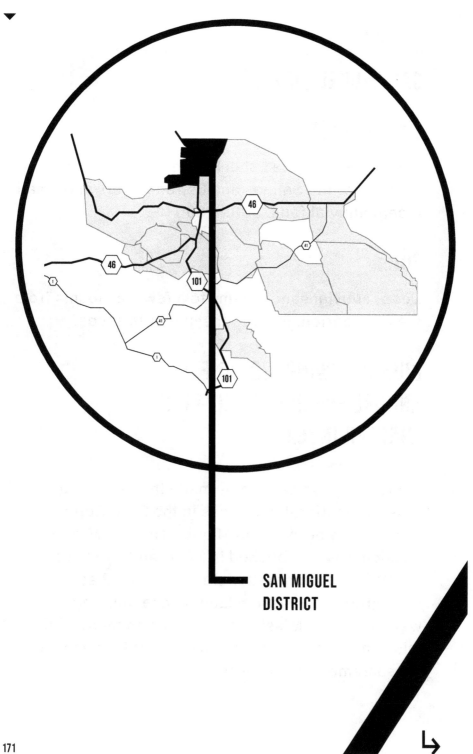

SAN MIGUEL
DISTRICT

SAN MIGUEL DISTRICT

TOPOGRAPHY:

Footslope of Santa Lucia Range, with alluvial terraces of the Salinas and Estrella rivers and small recent alluvial fans. 580-1,600 ft.

SOIL:

Deep, alluvial sandy loams to a few clay loams from the river bottom up onto the higher terraces.

DIURNAL SWING: 30-35°F
ANNUAL PRECIPITATION: 11.4"
WINKLER INDEX: III

There is a good case to be made that wine and other agricultural industries in the Paso Robles region were born in San Miguel. The San Miguel Mission was established in 1797, and by the early 1800s it was recorded that there were 19 acres of wine grapes on mission land. These plantings were likely the Mission grape, as with many of the missions, and it was used to make utilitarian wine for sacramental purposes.

There were 21 missions that stretched up the coast of California, typically spaced out to be approximately a one-day ride from each other by horseback. Each mission would, in essence, control the land surrounding it up to its border with the lands of the next mission.

The lands of the Mission San Miguel extended quite far beyond where today's town of San Miguel sits and mirror many of the characteristics of the Paso Robles region in general.

The mission district stretched west to the coastal mountain range all the way over to San Simeon, east to the far ranges that separated the central coast from the San Joaquin Valley, and south to what we call the Cuesta Grade today.

In 1822, land ownership changed hands when Mexico won its independence from Spain. Soon afterwards Mexico secularized the missions, changing the agricultural landscape forever.

Fast forward mid-century and the aftereffects of the gold rush, when many immigrant farmers and ranchers who did not strike it rich in the gold country made their way south and settled in San Luis Obispo County.

▼

The northern part of the county became an agricultural hub as would-be miners returned to their agricultural roots of raising cattle and growing crops, which of course included wine. Wine was very much a part of their cultures. Many came from France, Italy and Germany, and they brought local viticulture beyond the confines of the mission. Over several generations they transformed from farming grapes for their own use to commercial winemaking.

When the railroad made it to San Miguel in 1886, farmers and ranchers gained direct access to lucrative new sales channels, thus creating a boom.

Corrals complete with chutes and scales as well as grain elevators were built alongside the tracks. By 1887 there were 40 licensed businesses in San Miguel, and this northernmost town of San Luis Obispo County was home to the first newspaper in north county.

Unfortunately, agricultural prosperity was stifled when the region was hit with a drought in 1898.

▼

Most of California saw a vineyard planting boom in the late 1970s and early '80s, which was reflected in the Paso Robles region. Some of the more well-known vineyards in the San Miguel District were planted by Richard Sauret, who became revered throughout the region for his zinfandel.

As a third-generation north county resident, he grew up in viticulture. Sauret started tending vineyards in 1941 at the age of six and would go on to be a sought-after vineyard consultant.

In the '80s, David Caparone, after extensive research on clonal types and microclimates, decided to plant an experimental vineyard of nebbiolo in the San Miguel area.

Along with the first nebbiolo planted in the region, he would go on to plant sangiovese and aglianico, also firsts for Paso Robles.

Caparone is still in operation today as one of the oldest continuously owned and operated wineries in Paso Robles, dating back to 1979.

▼

The San Miguel District is the northwestern-most of the 11 AVAs of Paso Robles. Its northern boundary is the county line between Monterey and San Luis Obispo. It is bisected by the Salinas River, which flows to the north and empties into Monterey Bay. The Estrella River and Nacimiento River join the Salinas River within the San Miguel District. This naturally creates a setting of deep alluvial deposits of gravel, sand and silt.

The lowest elevation is just below 600 feet above sea level, rising to approximately 1,000 feet along various flood plains and river terraces. The District's western border is largely made up of steep mountains of the Santa Lucia range and the Camp Roberts military base. Its eastern edge lines up with the western edge of the Estrella District. The Adelaida District and the Estrella District stair-step the southern border.

The climate of the San Miguel District, compared to the rest of the Paso Robles AVA, is the windiest, warmest, and driest. (Portions of the easternmost AVAs could compete for this trifecta title as averages can vary.)

▼

The natural vegetation of the region reveals the growing conditions as there are scattered oaks across grassy hillsides and denser growths of trees and shrubs along the creek and river valleys where seasonal water flows.

The San Miguel District lies directly adjacent to the rain shadow of the Santa Lucia range, which can drastically reduce the amount of rainfall it receives.

There is also a lessened maritime influence in San Miguel, the result of its location near the higher northern range and outside of the window of the Templeton Gap effect to the south.

Many creeks and rivers dominate the landscape of the San Miguel District. The Salinas River Valley becomes quite wide through the area, and tributaries like San Marcos Creek, Peachy Creek and San Jacinto Creek add to the river-dominated landscape. Alluvial soils dominate the region and reflect the material's origins. Most vineyards are planted between 640 to 1,000 feet above sea level.

The soils at lower elevations can retain moisture. Higher elevations will have less topsoil on top of the bedrock, reducing vigor and elevating concentration. All in all, the climate and soils result in earlier maturation of fruit in the region.

▼

The San Miguel District is a foundational place for wine and indeed most agriculture in the Paso Robles region.

ALL AGRICULTURAL ACTIVITY IN NORTHERN SAN LUIS OBISPO COUNTY WAS SIGNIFICANTLY INFLUENCED BY THE MISSION SAN MIGUEL.

Just as influential was the change of governmental administration. Once Mexico took over the lands and secularized the mission, more homesteaders were allowed to plant their own deep roots in this agriculturally rich landscape.

Today, along with other crops and various livestock, wine grapes continue the long and fruitful tradition of agriculture in San Miguel.

▼

▼

TIN CITY

IN MANY CALIFORNIA WINE REGIONS, SUCCESS HAS COME AT A COST.

Smaller winemakers looking to open production facilities and tasting rooms have found themselves priced out of rapidly appreciating real estate markets. Rents in downtown neighborhoods are often beyond their reach.

And over the last decade, the tastes and habits of wine consumers have changed as well. Younger wine lovers are more interested in an intimate and casual experience that involves meeting the winemaker, seeing how wine is produced as they taste it, and experiencing wine as part of a larger sensory, aesthetic and gustatory experience.

The result has been the emergence of consumer-friendly wine neighborhoods in offbeat locations where the cost of building and operating a wine-making facility are more affordable, and where wineries are only one part of the scene.

▼

You can find them in Santa Barbara, Lompoc and — perhaps most successfully — in Paso Robles, where Tin City has set an impressive standard for the concept. An industrial neighborhood near the 101 a few miles south of Paso, home for many years to pool builders, air conditioning installers, auto repair shops and other unglamorous businesses, has transformed itself over the last decade into a haven for artisanal winemakers, distillers, brewers and several upscale businesses, including a a grocery store and a celebrated restaurant.

Young winemakers looking for a bargain-priced facility were the first to discover the neighborhood. In 2011, Andrew Jones envisioned it as the perfect spot for his new passion project, a winery he would call Field Recordings. "I was looking for something affordable and quiet. It was a good place for an upstart winery," Jones said in a 2021 interview with Pix.

A short while later, husband-and-wife team Brian and Stephanie Terrizzi signed a lease on a nearby building for their offbeat winery, Giornata. "In the beginning, everybody who started here was really nervous because we were small winemakers without much money, and we were all pretty young. But things took off pretty quickly," Terrizzi told Pix.

The metamorphosis continued in 2013 when BarrelHouse Brewing Co. opened the doors to its craft brewery and rambling gardens, where bands frequently perform on an impromptu stage – an old flatbed truck. You'll also find other very non-brewery touches, such as a fantastical artificial waterfall.

BarrelHouse and the small band of upstart winemakers established a beachhead, bringing thirsty crowds to the area for the first time, and it inspired a growing influx of artisanal winemakers and other related businesses. Many of them rented rustic spaces from Mike English, owner of a pool company who owned property in the area. New buildings popped up, imitating the rustic style of the original structures. Locals began calling the area Tin City, and the name stuck.

By the middle of the decade a second, larger wave of new tenants began arriving. "We always thought this was a really solid up-and coming-area, based on the success of (similar neighborhoods in) Lompoc and and Santa Barbara. it definitely had legs," said Jeff Strekas, director of operations and wine growing for ONX Wines. Its Tin City facility opened in 2015.

▼

Strekas likes the entrepreneurial spirit of Tin City and the mutual generosity of the winemakers that have taken up residence there. "There are a lot of synergies with wineries here. There's always a forklift right next door if you need one. We have the ability to help each other out and share equipment." That neighborliness also leads to exchanges of ideas as well — the upside of any shared work space where like-minded and ambitious people gather.

Some might grumble that Tin City has become too successful. Parking spaces can be hard to come by on the streets and lots that surround its 32 storefronts.

Mostly you'll find respected "garagiste" winemakers in residence here, but there's a healthy mix of other businesses as well: Tin City Cider Co., the super-popular restaurant Six Test Kitchen (in September 2021, it became the first restaurant in San Luis Obispo County to earn a Michelin star), Negranti Creamery, McPhee's Canteen, and Etto Pastificio, a gourmet Italian grocery run by Brian and Stephanie Terrizzi.

The feel of Tin City is industrial-chic with a touch of farmhouse. It's cozy and casual. Metal siding is the dominant building material, but its hard-edged look is softened by gentle pastel colors and the wineries' whimsical and imaginative logos. Some winemakers have indulged in flights of fancy in their designs. The tasting room at Field Recordings, for example, has been meticulously constructed to look like a high school gymnasium, down to amusing details such as team pennants and lockers lining the walls.

Murals and other works of art dot the Tin City landscape. Even the nearby railroad tracks seem to have been included in the design aesthetic. On some patios, you can watch passenger and freight trains whiz by just a few feet away.

But Tin City's biggest attraction is convenience. You can hit several tasting rooms, sip a craft beer for contrast, eat a great meal, and even do a little grocery shopping without getting into your car. "This is an area with lots of different things to do," Strekas said. "I think we do see a more diverse crowd here than at the winery, and it gives us the chance to introduce ourselves to people who otherwise might not be into wine culture."

▼

TIN CITY

Aaron
Anarchy Wine Co.
Anglim
Brian Benson Cellars
Cordant Winery
Desparada
Field Recordings
Giornata
Hubba Wines
Jocob Toft
Kaliedos
Levo Wine
Monochrome Wines
Nicora Wines
ONX Wines
Powell Mountain Cellars
Sans Liege Wines
Seven Oxen Winery
Turtle Rock
Two Moons
Union Sacre Winery

DOWNTOWN PASO

Cypher Winery
Derby Wine Estates
Hayseed and Housdon
Herman Story Wines
Indigené Cellars
LXV Wine
Pianetta Winery
Ranchero Cellars
Serial
Symbiosis Wines
Wine Boss Lounge

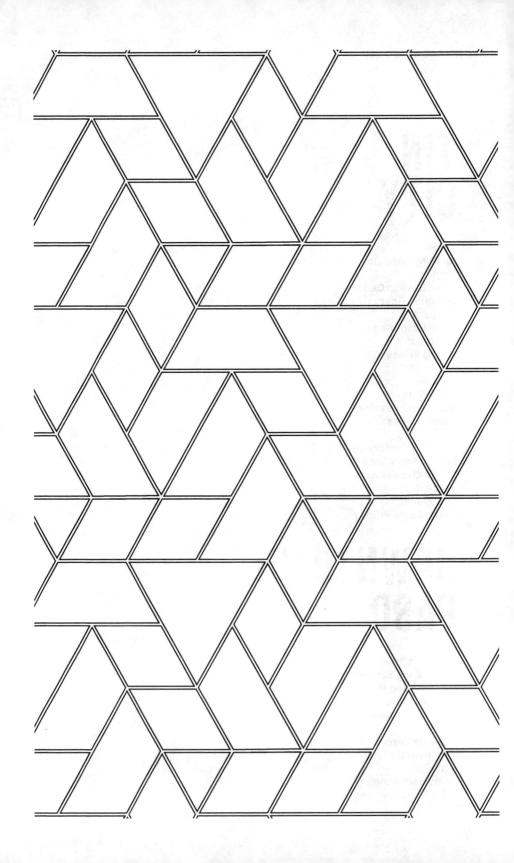

▼

CHAPTER

03:

WINEMAKER INTERVIEWS

WITH WINEMAKERS

INTERVIEWS

DRIVE THROUGH

Paso Robles has made a name for itself as a place that brings out the maverick spirit in the winemakers who work there.

These artisans embody the diversity, creativity and iconoclastic bent that has long defined the winemaking of Paso Robles.

In this chapter we talk to a several winemakers who represent the depth and diversity of Paso Robles, concentrating on the factors that distinguish their AVA.

▼

WINEMAKER

DANIEL DAOU

DAOU VINEYARDS

Born in Lebanon and raised in France, Daniel Daou learned to appreciate wine at an early age. His wine-loving father allowed him to taste Cheval Blanc and other classic French wines (cut with water, of course) when he was still a schoolboy.

Daou's love of computers brought him to the U.S. He settled in San Diego, where he and his brother Georges graduated from the University of California with degrees in electrical and computer engineering. After college, the brothers founded Daou Systems, a company that provides IT consulting and management services to the healthcare industry. It grew quickly in less than a decade, becoming one of 1997's top five initial public offerings in the country. Daniel "retired" at 31.

After selling his company, Daou jumped into winemaking. For eight years he made wine in his garage, learning the basics. His goal: to make great Bordeaux. He bid unsuccessfully on several promising properties in Northern California wine country before changing his focus to the Central Coast.

In 2007, Daou found the site he was looking for on Paso's hilly west side — part of the 1,200-acre property that had been owned by pioneer vintner Stanley Hoffman, who had planted the first Bordeaux grapes on the Central Coast in the early 1960s with impressive results.

From the beginning, Daou's wines have received a lot of attention, high scores and lavish praise from major wine critics. That's not surprising: Daou is obsessed with perfection in his cabernets and Bordeaux blends, and his winemaking methods include constant testing and phenolic analysis.

PAUL HODGINS:

What attracted you to this region west of Paso — the Adelaida AVA?

DANIEL DAOU:

It's the perfect place for Bordeaux. The reason why is because the temperature is perfect. The soil is perfect for growing. You don't want too much rocky soil for cabernet. The canopy doesn't grow well. Without a full canopy, cabernet does horribly. If you want to grow cab, you need clay.

HODGINS:

What do you like about the climate here?

DAOU:

One of the things you want to look for is how many days are 100° or more, because when the vine gets to 100°, it shuts down. You cook the grapes, you basically really impact the quality of the fruit. The east side, east of the 101, as well as downtown Paso, can be very hot. It sees on the average 30 to 40 days at 100° or more per year. Over here it's much cooler. How many days do you think we saw at 100° or more last year on our mountain? Zero. Not even one. We see on the average about five days at 100°.

HODGINS:

Why did it take a while for Paso to be accepted as a great producer of Bordeaux-style wines?

DAOU:

For the longest time it was fear. It was fear of competing with Napa and Bordeaux that held people back. It was fear to plant higher-elevation vineyards, to plant higher density vineyards, to

▼

plant better clones, to put more oak into it, to do the right thing when it comes to growth.

HODGINS:

What are the differences in taste profile between what you're doing at your location and what's happening at some of the better Napa winemakers?

DAOU:

The Paso cabs are going to have much more minerality because underneath the clay you have the limestone, so the roots penetrate that and actually draw those earthy mineral flavors straight into the glass. When you're tasting our wines, you're tasting 50/50 fruit to minerality. But because the climate is so beautiful, we're able to achieve ripeness before the wine sheds out some of this fruit intensity. Yes, you know, you're tasting a lot of the fruit. But then when it settles that minerality jumps out of the glass, and the layers and the complexity and the earth burst forth — to the point where it doesn't taste like a California cab. It tastes more like a Bordeaux, and a good vintage at that.

▼

HODGINS:

Is Bordeaux the wine of the future in Paso Robles?

DAOU:

Definitely. You know, those wines that tend to be a little higher alcohol, the traditional wines of Paso, there's a market for that. It's never going away, but it's absolutely shrinking and it will continue to shrink as cabernet takes over. When I started my Paso Robles CAB Collective in 2012, cabernet was at about 47% or 48% (of total acreage under vine) here. It's at 57% today after six, seven years, and it's growing every year. Every vineyard that I know around here is being planted to Bordeaux varieties.

HODGINS:

Will Paso eventually be as significant as Napa in the wine world?

▼

DAOU:

When I created the CAB Collective, I had one single goal in mind: I was going to change the mindset in Southern California. I want wine lovers down there to finally realize that you don't have to go to the airport, park your car, fly in an airplane, rent a car, drive two hours, stay in a hotel that costs 300 bucks a night, all to spend $300 on a bottle of wine that's probably not worth a third of that. You can come here instead, save a lot of time and money, and drink wonderful Bordeaux that has a personality all its own.

▼

WINE TASTER'S LOG

📅 Date of visit:

_____

🍷 Wines tasted:

_____   _____

_____   _____

📋 Notes:

_____

_____

_____

I met Daniel Daou and got his autograph!

_____

Daniel Daou

SHARE YOUR VISIT WITH US ON INSTAGRAM!

#DriveThroughPasoRobles
@Drive_Through_Books
@ilikethisgrape

▼

WINEMAKER

JANELL DUSI

J DUSI WINES

We profiled Janell earlier in this book. For the interview, we talked to her about her venerable family-owned winery's latest ventures, including the ambitious taming of rugged high-altitude terrain, which has produced a popular group of vineyards under the Paper Street label.

Paper Street was born in 2013, when Janell's father Mike Dusi discovered a 360-acre parcel of land in the northern part of Willow Creek AVA at an altitude of 2,200 feet. It was an unlikely place to establish a vineyard: hilly, rocky and long neglected. And it contained some oddities, including an ancient olive orchard and an abandoned observatory.

For three years Mike toiled with his sons Matt and Michael, hauling away dead trees with bulldozers, clearing the land of boulders and rocks, often by hand, and planting a vineyard. It was painstaking and labor-intensive work. Only 110 of the 360 acres could be cultivated, and they were far from easy to tame: steep, treacherous, and dotted with limestone outcroppings.

Over the next few years the plantings grew.

Current Paper Street varieties include zinfandel, mourvedre, grenache, syrah, grenache blanc, tempranillo, carignane, cabernet sauvignon, clairette, and petite sirah. The first official vintage was 2016.

PAUL HODGINS:

Tell us a bit about Paper Street.

JANELL DUSI:

Paper Street is mostly Willow Creek (AVA) and maybe one-eighth in Adelaida. The most important factor influencing the grapes is elevation. This is one of the highest places in the region where grapes are grown. The altitude influences temperature especially.

HODGINS:

Paper Street has been producing for five years now. What have you discovered about it that surprised you?

▼

DUSI:

I think one of the craziest things we did is we took some old Dante Dusi (Janell's grandfather) zinfandel cuttings, put them on rootstock and planted them up there just to see what would happen, and we were shocked by how vastly different the fruit is.

It's the same clone, the same everything, but planted at twice the elevation. It's in a more temperate climate with steep hillsides and rocky calcareous stone, which affects drainage. That fruit, when it drops on the crush pad, is a different beast: darker, with a thicker skin. To see it be as dark and intense as it is, that's phenomenal. We've been on steep learning curves with other varietals in terms of farming practices. It's just windy and wild and intense.

HODGINS:

What is the effect of this location on the grapes grown there?

DUSI:

We know that the vineyards near Paper Street, Law and Daou, they're producing top-quality fruit. There's something about stressing out these vines on those steep hillsides. It produces thicker skins, smaller berries.

HODGINS:

I've heard it's challenging to work up there.

DUSI:

It's crazy to get even 100 acres harvested. We've rented goose-neck trailers and special trucks to deal with the terrain. We're still an Old School farming family. My dad is up there from sunup to sundown. He's on his second knee replacement. There's a dangerous aspect to it. We lost some equipment; someone lost part of a finger. Paper Street wears the guys out so much faster. We started night harvesting up there this year; you can't work during the day on those hills in the heat. No wheeled tractors are allowed up there because of the steep hillsides. Other (Dusi) vineyards have been handed down over the generations. This is the first time we've tried seeking out a piece of raw land and figuring out what varieties to plant.

HODGINS:

How did you choose what to grow up there?

DUSI:

If you sign contracts with us, we will plant what you want. We still sell 80 percent of what we grow. We've always been big sellers. Years ago we sold to large names like Paul Masson and Ridge.

HODGINS:

There's been a tremendous influx of people from other parts of the state lately to this area. Why are they coming?

DUSI:

People are now buying up houses like mad and retiring in wine country — folks from Los Angeles and San Francisco. We are getting a lot of Napa guys coming down to buy fruit now. They're looking for anything interesting. And we're getting winemakers from other areas who like the approach here. Paso has that Wild West atmosphere where you can make anything you want and do whatever you feel like as a winemaker.

What the Napa guys have discovered is the fruit is less expensive but the quality is there. It's interesting to see who's coming around and knocking on doors.

HODGINS:

Now that Paper Street is producing, what's your next big project?

DUSI:

I've done a lot of thinking about the five-year plan. I've thought about expanding to a bigger production facility and growing my distribution. I've finally decided that for me and my preferred stress level, I'm at a good spot right now. I want to spend more time on the wine side, and not make more wine but just make better wine. I'm really happy; I work my butt off every day. I like being the one who travels to Idaho and Montana to sell wine. I love talking about me and my family.

HODGINS:

How did the pandemic change your business?

▼

DUSI:

We did invest some money in the outside area at the tasting room. We bought some heaters. Outdoor tasting is the new future. It's proven to be a cool new way to do our tasting. We're spread out across the grounds now. You have a server talking to you about the wines. And now that reservations are getting to be more the norm, people have to think about where they're going. It has elevated the experience. And I think that's a great thing.

▼

WINE TASTER'S LOG

📅 Date of visit:

🍷 Wines tasted:

📋 Notes:

I met Janell Dusi and got her autograph!

Janell Dusi

SHARE YOUR VISIT WITH US
ON INSTAGRAM!

#DriveThroughPasoRobles
@Drive_Through_Books
@ilikethisgrape

WINEMAKER

GARY EBERLE

EBERLE WINERY

Gary Eberle was born and raised in Moon Township, Penn., 12 miles northwest of Pittsburgh, into a hardscrabble working-class household. He was raised by a single mom.

Football was Eberle's escape. Already burly and athletic in middle school, he had become an excellent football player by his teens. He attended Penn State and played defensive tackle under legendary coach Joe Paterno.

After graduating with a bachelor's in biology, Eberle attended Louisiana State University, where he studied cellular genetics. It was there that his aversion to quality alcoholic beverages finally was conquered.

One of Eberle's professors introduced him to fine French wine, which led to an epiphany. Forsaking his studies, he went to UC Davis to pursue his doctorate in fermentation science. He moved to Paso two years later, drawn by its potential for cabernet sauvignon.

Eberle cofounded Estrella River Winery & Vineyards in 1973, and it turned into a major winery. By the late '70s he was itching to strike out on his own, so he acquired 64 acres close by. His 1979 cabernet sauvignon featured the now familiar boar logo. It's a playful reference to the German origin of the name Eberle, which means "small boar." An iron boar fountain — a popular Paso icon — marks the entrance to Eberle's tasting room.

 From the beginning, Eberle established a reputation for quality and vision, and his long career is a succession of firsts. In 1975 he planted the first substantial syrah vineyard in California and sold the state's first 100% syrah. Eberle was one of the cofounders of the Paso Robles AVA in 1983. In 1994 he expanded underground, building the first wine caves in Paso Robles.

PAUL HODGINS:

As a doctoral student at UC Davis, you came down to Paso in the early '70s with your professors. What was it that impressed you about Paso way back then?

▼

GARY EBERLE:

I came down here on three different trips with my professors and a couple of trips on my own, but the thing I think that really solidified it was the feedback from all my professors. They said that Paso Robles will be the next great red wine producing region in the United States. So I got down here to make red wine right in time for the white wine revolution. Perfect timing.

HODGINS:

You must have had the area pretty much to yourself back then.

EBERLE:

When I came down to Paso Robles, there were three real wineries. All of them had been here since the repeal of Prohibition. The next technically trained winemakers didn't show up for another five years. It was 20 years before things really started. Once our wines got good and sound year after year after year, that's when the media really started paying attention to Paso Robles. Then there was an influx of trained winemakers and winemakers who had not only gotten a fancy degree, but had apprenticed at

▼

two or three good wineries. And that's when you saw the big explosion of quality wine.

HODGINS:

Your goal was always to produce big reds.

EBERLE:

To make great cabernet, that was what I was seeking. And I knew even then that I couldn't afford to play the game in Napa or Sonoma but I could in Paso Robles. At that time, I could get really good land at prices I could afford.

HODGINS:

You got interested in syrah after spending some time in Australia. Tell us about your first planting of syrah and your experience with the grape.

EBERLE:

I have the single oldest planting of syrah in the United States. But it's a labor of love, not profit. One of the big problems with syrah is people aren't willing to pay as much for Rhône wines as they will for cabernet.

▼

HODGINS:

You're known as one of the most sociable winemakers in Paso. I see you in the tasting room all the time.

EBERLE:

I love wine and I drink wine every day, but even more than the wine, I love the social part of wine, having a glass of wine with friends. I sit up front with the public like Mr. Mondavi used to; he taught me to do that.

HODGINS:

What do you think of the West side/East side divide?

EBERLE:

It's deceptive. The West side has the hottest vineyards and the coldest vineyards, the highest elevation and the lowest elevation. The most rainfall and the least rainfall are in vineyards in the West side. And the soil is very fractured and diverse. The only thing unique about the West side is it is very pretty. There are great wines being produced all over this appellation, whether it's Geneseo, Adelaida,

▼

Willow Creek, Estrella, Creston, El Pomar, Templeton Gap. What's important is who's farming it. I pay much more attention to that than the location of the vineyard.

HODGINS:

How does your approach to making big reds differ from Napa winemakers?

EBERLE:

There's a lot of oak tannin that the people in Napa are very proud of. They love their brand new French oak. But I don't think that's really all that attractive. I want to taste the grape. That was drummed into me at UC Davis, and from Mr. Mondavi too. He used to say your job was to take the grapes, put them into the bottle, and do as little damage to them as you can along the way. Homo sapiens like fruit. I try to give them as much fruit as I can.

WINE TASTER'S LOG

Date of visit:

_____

Wines tasted:

_____   _____

_____   _____

Notes:

_____

_____

_____

I met Gary Eberle and got his autograph!

_____

Gary Eberle

SHARE YOUR VISIT WITH US ON INSTAGRAM!

#DriveThroughPasoRobles
@Drive_Through_Books
@ilikethisgrape

WINEMAKER

GUILLAUME FABRE

CLOS SOLÈNE

Guillaume Fabre's family has made wine for many generations. Born in Narbonne, France, he worked from an early age with his father in the Languedoc-Roussillon region before following him to a new project in Bordeaux.

Fabre pursued a major in winemaking, enology and vineyard management at the Lycée Charlemagne in Carcassonne, graduating in 2001. He was thrust into his first career job at 21, managing a winery following the unexpected death of its owner.

After two years Fabre had the property running smoothly, and the family re-assumed control. At that point he left France for America. Fabre had heard about Stephan Asseo, the brilliant winemaker who had gotten Robert Parker's attention with his French-style wines at L'Aventure, the Paso winery he founded in 1997. Asseo brought the young Frenchman on as an intern.

Fabre stayed for 10 years and became assistant winemaker. On the side, he made his own wine, experimenting on a site close to L'Aventure called Russell Family Vineyard. Finally, in 2007, Fabre was ready to launch his own label, Clos Solène, named after his wife. His winery's vineyards are in the heart of the Willow Creek District, between his former home, L'Aventure, and one of Paso's most celebrated wineries, Saxum.

Solène asked her husband to start by making something she could enjoy with food. Their first wine was a roussanne, a Rhône white that he remembers fondly from his childhood. His wines consistently score highly with critics. Clos Selene's 2017 Harmonie Red, a Rhône blend, received a 95-point score from *Wine Enthusiast*.

PAUL HODGINS:

You started in France and spent the first part of your career making wines in two of its iconic regions. What was it like adjusting to Paso?

GUILLAUME FABRE:

When I got here I decided it was definitely an approach to winemaking that I could learn. I had to adjust my attitude and learn about how different it is: weather, soil, how to protect the clusters from the heat or frost. It took me six, seven years to really adjust myself. By 2015 or '16 I was really finding my own style.

▼

HODGINS:

What are the most significant differences between the wines of Napa and those of Paso Robles?

FABRE:

The soils of Napa can be much more volcanic and those wines are getting riper and riper. And then there is less and less acid. I believe that Bordeaux and other (big reds) need a little bit of acidity, which is maybe my French side coming through.

HODGINS:

What's your stand on the rule-breaking "Paso blend"?

FABRE:

I think we have the capacity to do it, and it makes us distinctive. There are so many varietals that do very well here. But the problem, you know, is that Napa is very narrowly focused, which from a (marketing) point of view is quite important. Here you can make a great syrah or a grenache-syrah-mourvèdre or a completely unique blend that combines some cabernet and a Rhône grape and some zinfandel.

And you have people like Matt Trevisan and other talented winemakers who can blend very different grapes together really nicely. I'm a little bit more traditional. I do a little bit of a Paso blend, but generally I'm much more straightforward and I don't cross-blend much. I think we can lose our identity if we just blend without putting thought or tradition behind it.

HODGINS:

Compared to Napa or any other wine region in California, Paso is so much bigger. Does it have the potential to expand even more, or are we reaching the limit of what water and other resources can support?

FABRE:

There's still a lot of land undeveloped, and I see a very big influence of people from Napa going to Paso and more brands coming, more high-end winemaking. So I think we'll see more planting. But you're right about the (shortage of) water, especially on the East side. When people have money, it's easy to buy whatever you want.

▼

I'm concerned about a lot of people coming here, but I don't want to be selfish about it. There's still a lot of room to grow if we do it intelligently and mindfully.

HODGINS:

You mentioned money. Some deep-pockets investors have come into Paso over the last few years and really built some very impressive wineries. What are the upsides and downsides of that?

FABRE:

I think it's a great thing on balance, you know, because those people for the most part have been acting responsibly and trying to preserve and cherish what we have here. Some people have made a few mistakes, but I feel that they have learned and want to act responsibly and in the best interests of the region.

HODGINS:

Is there still room for artisanal winemakers? Do they still have a place in Paso? Is quality winemaking still doable on an intimate scale?

▼

FABRE:

Yeah, I think so. If you have a very strong perception of what you want to do and the desire to go in one focused direction, I think it's doable. If it's only to come to make some unremarkable wine and to be in the middle of the pool, then it's going to be difficult. You have to find an audience that appreciates what you're doing and is willing to support you over the long run.

▼

WINE TASTER'S LOG

📅 Date of visit:

🍷 Wines tasted:

📋 Notes:

I met Guillaume Fabre and got his autograph!

Guillaume Fabre

SHARE YOUR VISIT WITH US
ON INSTAGRAM!

#DriveThroughPasoRobles
@Drive_Through_Books
@ilikethisgrape

Q & A

WINEMAKER

JORDAN FIORENTINI

EPOCH ESTATE WINES

Jordan Fiorentini brings an impressive level of scientific training to her winemaking: a bachelor's degree in engineering from Dartmouth College and a master's degree in viticulture from UC Davis.

But there's an artistic side to Fiorentini as well. An accomplished painter, she tries to capture on canvas the qualities and personality of the wines she makes. Her whimsical works look Dali-esque, but they're serious attempts to express her wine's essence.

Fiorentini's father made wine in her native Georgia, and she learned the basics by working with him. She also discovered that she loved winemaking. After earning her viticulture degree, Fiorentini worked at Araujo Estate Wines in Napa Valley, at Antinori Winery in Italy (where she met her Italian husband), and as head winemaker at Sonoma County's esteemed Chalk Hill.

Fiorentini enjoys working at one of the Central Coast's most historic wineries. Epoch occupies the former site of Ascension, the first winery in the area. Her appreciation of history extends to winemaking techniques as well. She has experimented with amphorae (clay vessels)

▼

which winemakers used before the time of Christ. Fiorentini is also interested in the "Paso blend" — unorthodox blends of grapes from different regions. For example, her 2013 Estate blend combines classic Rhône varieties —grenache, syrah and mourvèdre — with tempranillo and zinfandel.

PAUL HODGINS:

Tell us a little bit about the York Mountain AVA. It's much cooler than Paso, right?

JORDAN FIORENTINI:

Yeah. You get the maritime influence; it's breezy and windy up here all the time. Today the wind is blowing and the fog is rolling in and it's damp. Whereas it's probably not wet at all in Templeton and Paso right now. Some years are foggier than others; some are cooler than others. But whatever the vintage is, on a hot day we're 10 to 20° cooler than Paso. And then on a cool day we're much, much cooler and the sun might not come out. So there's those factors, and then there's so much more rainfall. So I think Paso might have 15 inches annually and we'll have 35 to 50.

▼

HODGINS:

So dry farming is a real possibility up there.

FIORENTINI:

It is the only thing we could do because there's no groundwater. We've tried. We have one well on the property. It services all the buildings. It's not enough for the vineyard, even when the vines were babies. And so we just had to dry farm, we didn't have a choice. We weren't sure what was going to happen, but because of the good rainfall and probably less intensity of heat, even the baby vines were okay.

HODGINS:

Is the soil calcareous there like it is throughout much of Paso's West side?

FIORENTINI:

For us, I'm not saying there's not a tiny bit of calcareous soil in the York Mountain AVA, but we're all sandstone. It's also really well drained.

HODGINS:

Tell me about the discussions you and Epoch founder-owner Bill Armstrong had about what grapes to plant up here a decade ago.

FIORENTINI:

2010 was my first year here. When he and I started talking about it, 2012, 2013, we were both fixed on the same philosophy: we don't believe you should grow every variety just because you can. We wanted to focus and get good at what we knew, and also what you think is right for the area. We were thinking about Rhône when we started. Bill was really excited about the cooler climate being appropriate for viognier that would be Condrieu-like. I was really excited for syrah potentially. But we weren't sure if it was going to be warm enough here, you know?

HODGINS:

What else did Bill want to plant?

▼

FIORENTINI:

Bill wanted cabernet up here. He wanted a tiny bit of cabernet. He and Justin Smith had talked about that years ago. So we've had this little sliver of cabernet, and on the lowest part of the hillside a little bit of zinfandel.

HODGINS:

How did the cabernet sauvignon turn out?

FIORENTINI:

It's super peppery green, but I love that character when it's done well, because I want to know when I'm drinking a cabernet that it tastes like a cabernet.

HODGINS:

Tell me about the specific qualities common to York Mountain wines.

FIORENTINI:

York Mountain AVA wine has a lot of great acidity, and it's got just this full, fleshy fruit. And you'll notice a lot more spice element to the wines right off the bat.

▼

And there's just this different play on the quality of fruit. Maybe it doesn't have as much of that sweet extract as you would get from many Paso wines, but then it's got a delicious and complex spice. It's just a different palette from wines further east.

HODGINS:

What is this region's best quality compared to other wine areas of California?

FIORENTINI:

There's longer hang time here so we're not forced to pick based on sugar or weather. So I think our wines might develop better over time; the good, more extractable tannins come out more easily.

▼

WINE TASTER'S LOG

📅 Date of visit:

_____

🍷 Wines tasted:

_____ _____

_____ _____

📋 Notes:

_____

_____

_____

I met Jordan Fiorentini and got her autograph!

_____

Jordan Fiorentini

SHARE YOUR VISIT WITH US ON INSTAGRAM!

#DriveThroughPasoRobles
@Drive_Through_Books
@ilikethisgrape

▼

WINEMAKER

AUSTIN
HOPE

HOPE FAMILY WINES

Austin Hope moved from Bakersfield to Paso Robles with his family as a child in 1978. His parents Chuck and Marilyn had purchased some ranch land and they intended to plant apple orchards and grape vineyards. Chuck soon determined that Paso Robles was better for grapes than apples, and by the early '80s the vineyards were productive.

The Hopes sold their grapes to various wine producers through the rest of that decade and into the '90s. Buyers included the renowned Wagner family, owners of Napa Valley's Caymus Vineyards, who purchased cabernet sauvignon grapes for their Liberty School label.

Austin worked in the vineyards with his dad, the beginning of a lifelong fascination with the science and art of wine.

He studied fruit science at California Polytechnic State University in nearby San Luis Obispo and taking advantage of family connections, worked in Napa Valley under Chuck Wagner, Caymus' widely respected winemaker.

▼

Austin graduated from Cal Poly in 1996 with a Bachelor of Science and helped his family make the transition from grape producers to winemakers.

That year, the Hopes purchased the Liberty School label from the Wagners and launched Treana Winery, where Austin served as assistant winemaker under Chris Phelps. He became principal winemaker two years later.

In 2000 the Hope family launched the Austin Hope label, which focused exclusively on estate-grown Rhône varieties.

In 2008, the Hope family introduced Candor Wines, focusing on zinfandel and merlot sourced from family-owned vineyards in Santa Barbara Paso Robles and Lodi.

It introduced its second multi-vintage blend, Troublemaker, in 2010.

▼

PAUL HODGINS:

What was the wine industry in Paso like when your family arrived in 1978?

AUSTIN HOPE:

Back then there was probably, I don't know, half a dozen real wineries, if that; maybe a thousand acres of grapes. You fast forward to today and it's like geez, Louise. It's changed dramatically for sure.

HODGINS:

You were an early proponent of dividing the Paso Robles AVA. Tell us about that.

HOPE:

Justin Smith and I were kind of what started this whole sub-AVA thing. Years ago, we felt that this Templeton Gap area, which is where our estate vineyard is and the tasting cellar is, was something that was special and unique

▼

concerning Rhône varietals. And so we hired a guy to help us. And one of our buddies flew us around in his little plane to kind of survey the area. You know, we weren't as sophisticated as we are today, but this was a long time ago. And we put together a proposal to (the Alcohol and Tobacco Tax and Trade Bureau) and they basically laughed at us. It was like a one-page deal. They said, "You guys are crazy. You have to be scientific about it!" But it motivated people to take an interest in it and we got the ball rolling.

HODGINS:

You and others who have spent their lives here had pretty strong convictions about where the dividing lines should be, correct?

HOPE:

I was a farmer my whole life here and in winemaking for a better part of my life at that point. And we knew where the soils were best for Rhônes and for cabernet. We've spent a decade or more completely analyzing the soils in those particular areas. And we've gotten to know the climate very well. Templeton Gap is the coldest sub-AVA within the whole region.

HODGINS:

You also believe that certain varieties can vary a lot according to the sub-AVA they're grown in.

HOPE:

Our syrahs that we grow here will be more like Northern Rhône syrahs. They'll be more Côte-Rôtie. There's more structure to them; they'll have the blueberries and meat and smoke kind of qualities. But if you go out east past the Estrella District and into the Highlands, out in that area it's much warmer. Syrah from out there is more like a shiraz. It's more bubblegum flavors, less structure, more weight.

HODGINS:

The West side certainly gets a lot of attention. Are there distinctions among those West side AVAs that we could really notice when we open a bottle of wine from Templeton Gap versus Willow Creek or Adelaida?

HOPE:

The Eastern portion of Willow Creek is fairly similar to Templeton Gap. Overall, though,

▼

(Willow Creek is) a little bit warmer. I think our Rhônes would be similar, but there are some spots in Willow Creek that are warmer that do well with cabernet. The Adelaida District is a completely different district. Tablas Creek (Vineyard) chose that area because it's warmer. They were trying to match the Châteauneuf-du-Pape region of Southern Rhône. If you drew a straight line it would take you only half an hour from here to there, but it's twice the amount of rainfall that we have here, really different soils, and much hotter.

HODGINS:

So much has been written and talked about concerning the West side. But of course there are people like Steve Peck over at J. Lohr and Gary Eberle and others who have been making great wine from the East side for quite a while. Do you think it's a little underdeveloped or under-appreciated compared to the areas west of the 101?

HOPE:

Absolutely. When I was growing up the old adage was you talk about the West side and you grow on the East side. And I think why the West side got so much more notice is because early on there were more high-quality wines coming out of the West side than the East side. Justin was one of those but a lot of us get a lot of our fruit from the East side. There's no denying the fact that we're huge East side advocates. I think there's no question that there's more high-quality soils and acreage for cabernet on the East side than there ever will be on the West side.

WINE TASTER'S LOG

Date of visit:

Wines tasted:

Notes:

I met Austin Hope and got his autograph!

Austin Hope

SHARE YOUR VISIT WITH US
ON INSTAGRAM!

#DriveThroughPasoRobles
@Drive_Through_Books
@ilikethisgrape

▼

WINEMAKER

STEVE PECK

J. LOHR VINEYARDS & WINES

Growing up in Ventura County, Steve Peck visited his uncle to help out with harvest each fall, taking the 101 north along the coast to Santa Cruz. Usually his family would stop at the Pesenti Winery in Paso Robles to fill up their gallon jugs with old-vine zinfandel straight from giant oak casks. Peck was impressed by the joy his parents took in that annual tradition.

As a young man, Peck was drawn to the food and wine movement, and he took every opportunity to get involved. One summer, just before transferring to UC Davis for his junior year, he worked the crush at Joseph Phelps in Napa Valley.

At the beginning of Peck's career in 1986, the wine economy was depressed. But with a degree in chemical engineering, Peck knew he would be employable elsewhere.

For decades, Peck worked in biotech for Smucker's, Merck and Genencor International. But every year he still made wine in his garage. By 2001, Peck was fermenting 10 barrels a year with his uncle and a group of friends. He kept up all his old relationships at Phelps and other wineries up and down the California coast.

▼

Peck finally changed careers when he joined Five Rivers Winery as winemaker in 2001. Peck worked in Monterey County, Paso Robles and Santa Barbara County, and he helped manage harvest scheduling for dozens of growers.

During this part of his career, Peck's reputation as a master of red wines began to grow. He became one of the most well-liked and well-respected winemakers on the Central Coast. In 2007 Peck took over red wine production at J. Lohr, employing his considerable talents to guide one of the most successful wineries in California.

PAUL HODGINS:

How would you describe the Paso region geographically to first-time visitors who don't know it?

STEVE PECK:

I always think of Paso Robles as an elevated valley. It's bordered on three sides by hills and open to the north. To the south, Santa Margarita Lake is the headwaters for the Salinas River, which flows through the center of everything from south to north up to Monterey Bay. The mountains on the west side of Paso, the Santa Lucia Range, form the western boundary, and to some degree they form the southern boundary as well.

HODGINS:

Tell me how the area is affected by the maritime influence through the Templeton Gap.

PECK:

It's almost like a thermal rainbow. Instead of being a long strip of air, it's more of a fan or a slice of pizza or something like that. And you go through those bandwidths of temperature drop. There are two sub-AVAs that are closest, Willow Creek and Templeton Gap District, that are most affected by that cool air source. But it spreads out north and east, and its effect is felt over much of the area.

HODGINS:

The AVA designations are fairly new. How much do we know about some of these regions?

PECK:

You know, in a lot of cases there aren't even initially wineries identified with those regions. And I know for J. Lohr in particular, some of these locations aren't well understood yet. It is sometimes a challenge to talk about the characteristics of an AVA. We'll know more a few years down the road.

HODGINS:

Even with its present sub-AVAs, there's a lot of diversity within regions, isn't there?

PECK:

For sure. Adelaida is one of the most diverse regions. It's got a wide variety of soils and temperature variations. There are some pretty hot parts to Adelaida and pockets where things are entirely different from what's close by.

HODGINS:

You source your grapes from many different areas around Paso, don't you?

PECK:

Pretty much everything J. Lohr does is Region II and III. We're in Adelaida, in El Pomar, San Miguel. And we have some high elevation stuff out there at Creston. We're up at over 1,700 feet there.

▼

HODGINS:

As a Bordeaux producer, what are the differences between Paso and Napa Bordeaux wines, in your opinion?

PECK:

I would say that Paso wines tend to be less tannic. And I would say that the winemakers here have become more careful about making sure that we are not allowing overripe flavors have their way. I look back to one of the most severe drought vintages, 2004, and there were a lot of high-alcohol wines that year that were really sexy in the barrel room six months after harvest, but the wine didn't age very well, you know? So the best winemakers are using methods to get rid of pyrazines during the summer by creating that water deficit through June, July, August. They're not relying only on hang time so that we are in the correct Brix window and flavor window for our fruit character.

HODGINS:

How has the influx of large, well-financed wineries changed Paso in the time that you've been here?

▼

PECK:

I think it has changed, you know, but it's changed things for the better. When that kind of wealth hit Napa Valley winemaking in the 1970s, it really staved off the housing developments and the Wal-Marts and all that other typical development from just continuing to march north up the valley, and it created a special lifestyle and experience for not only the locals, but for the global community. It turned Napa Valley as a whole into a destination. I think wealth in the wine industry can serve the community for the better.

▼

WINE TASTER'S LOG

📅 Date of visit:

_____

🍷 Wines tasted:

_____   _____

_____   _____

📋 Notes:

_____

_____

_____

I met Steve Peck and got his autograph!

_____

Steve Peck

SHARE YOUR VISIT WITH US ON INSTAGRAM!

#DriveThroughPasoRobles
@Drive_Through_Books
@ilikethisgrape

▼

WINEMAKER

VICTOR HUGO ROBERTS

VICTOR HUGO WINERY

Victor Hugo Winery, a rustic spread near the border of the Templeton Gap and El Pomar AVAs, looks much like it did when Victor Hugo Roberts first opened his doors to the public almost 25 years ago. The tasting room is two barrels and a board in a large, old barn filled with Roberts' wine in various stages of aging.

Victor Hugo is a classic example of the small, family-owned and operated wineries that used to dominate the area around Paso Robles. Roberts remembers when cattle were king (his own vineyards lie on a former cattle ranch).

Roberts arrived in Paso Robles three years after receiving his enology degree from U.C. Davis in 1979. In 1982 he accepted a position as winemaker and general manager at Creston, owned by TV game show host Alex Trebek. But the dream of striking out on his own consumed Roberts.

In 1985 Vick and his wife Leslie planted 15 acres on the Templeton property which today is the site of the family home and winery, housed in a century-old barn.

▼

More vineyards were added through the years, and Vick and Leslie now farm 78 acres of chardonnay, zinfandel, syrah, petite sirah, viognier, cabernet sauvignon, cabernet franc, merlot, malbec and petit verdot. Victor Hugo's first vintage was released in 1999, the year the tasting room opened to the public.

PAUL HODGINS:

What was the attitude in other parts of the California wine world about Paso Robles when you first arrived?

VICTOR HUGO ROBERTS:

Not particularly respectful. The wisdom from some of the other regions was that it was too hot to grow wine grapes here. It's true that in certain areas the warmest summer days can be well above 100°, but large parts of Paso may only have three or four days that hit that temperature.

What the region has that sets it apart is the huge diurnal temperature swing — that 45- to 50-degree temperature change after sundown. I think that's the biggest thing that everyone was overlooking.

▼

HODGINS:

Some people say Paso is a great Rhône area. Others say it's better for Bordeaux. What's your position?

ROBERTS:

I think the areas that generally have the most upside potential are those with calcareous formations, fractured shale and limestone soils. That geology runs northwest to southeast, but doesn't encompass the entire region. It includes most of Templeton Gap, Willow Creek, much of Adelaida, and to a smaller degree York Mountain.

Not to say that you can't grow top quality grapes in different soil structure. One of the things that we have proven here is that with proper vineyard management, you can grow top quality grapes in a number of different soil types. Rocky, well-drained soils are ideal, but people certainly have made very nice wines out of areas that don't have that much rock in them.

HODGINS:

Are there specific taste profiles to different sub-AVAs in Paso?

ROBERTS:

I think there are some subtle differences. If every grower grew 3.5 tons to the acre, and they were all on vertical shoot positioning, all grown and harvested at the same Brix, there'd be more uniformity of taste. The decisions about when to harvest and how to farm are huge. Templeton Gap wines tend to have slightly lower alcohols and slightly higher acidities, but it's tough to really make subtle distinctions because of the winemaking input and harvest parameters.

HODGINS:

Will Paso ever have the rigor and varietal focus of Napa?

ROBERTS:

Part of Paso's charm, and part of what has attracted a lot of people here, is the idea that winemakers have a lot of latitude to grow whatever they want.

▼

I think it's a good thing that we don't have uniformity of varietals. Whole areas of Napa Valley are nothing but cab or Bordeaux blenders. And Carneros is almost exclusively chardonnay and pinot noir. That really hasn't happened in Paso.

HODGINS:

Do you think Paso's East side/West side split is too simplistic?

ROBERTS:

The 101 divide. Of course. The last time I looked I didn't see the wind stopping right at the 101. Part of the reasons for forming the 11 sub-AVAs is that winemakers here long ago realized the region is much more complex than east-west. The warmest area in the whole AVA is actually west of San Miguel. The areas that are dominated by or very closely aligned with the Templeton Gap are the coolest areas, regardless of where they are in relation to east and west.

HODGINS:

What are Paso's greatest strengths as a wine region?

▼

ROBERTS:

Paso Robles is one of the three best areas in the state to grow zinfandel. Paso Robles zin has the potential for being top notch, year in and year out. The secret is to get it ripe, but not overripe. Because it 's an early to mid-season ripening grape, you have the potential to get it very ripe in Paso's climate. And I would say that the blends that have been created are an indication of some of the creativity of people in the region. They're not worried about, "Well, those two aren't ever blended together." Well they are around here.

WINE TASTER'S LOG

📅 Date of visit:
_____

🍷 Wines tasted:

_____   _____

_____   _____

📋 Notes:

_____

_____

_____

I met Victor Hugo Roberts and got his autograph!

_____

Victor Hugo Roberts

SHARE YOUR VISIT WITH US ON INSTAGRAM!

#DriveThroughPasoRobles
@Drive_Through_Books
@ilikethisgrape

▼

WINEMAKER

JUSTIN SMITH

SAXUM VINEYARDS

Justin Smith rocketed to fame in one fell swoop. His winery's 2007 James Berry Vineyard Paso Robles Rhône blend was named *Wine Spectator's* 2010 Wine of the Year — No. 1 in the world. Wine tastemaker Robert Parker was also impressed, awarding it 100 points. "Utter perfection, and one of the most profound Rhône Ranger wines I have ever tasted," he announced.

Smith's father, James, a San Diego County veterinarian, bought the James Berry property in what is now the Willow Creek District when Justin was 10. Pebble, as Justin's dad was known, started creating a vineyard right away, doing even the most physically taxing work himself. Meanwhile, Justin spent many happy hours zipping around the property on his bike.

Pebble ended up working for Fetzer Vineyards, selling most of his annual yield to them, and became the winery's representative for the Central Coast.

But watching their grapes disappear into someone else's wine was discouraging.

▼

In the late 1980s, the family made a crucial decision to change direction and produce their own wine. Encouraged by local winemaker John Alban, Pebble planted mourvèdre and viognier, then syrah. In 1995, the Smiths purchased another 20 acres, and by this time the die was cast: They planted nothing but Rhône grapes on the new property.

Justin, already a knowledgeable winemaker in his teens, attended Cal Poly in nearby San Luis Obispo. After graduating, he came back to manage the family vineyard. As payment, his father presented Justin with one block of syrah. Together with his college housemate, Matt Trevisan, Justin used the fruit to start the Linne Calodo winery; the pair's first vintage was 300 cases.

After a few years they parted ways, and Smith formed his own winery, Saxum, on the family land in the Willow Creek district. Despite his success, and the addition of a large cave on the property, Smith intends to keep his output small and his quality high.

▼

PAUL HODGINS:

You were one of the winemakers who helped determine the 11 sub-AVAs of Paso. Tell us a bit about the thinking that went into it, especially on the West side.

JUSTIN SMITH:

When we drew out the AVAs, there were three kind of distinct areas of the West side: Adelaida, Willow Creek and Templeton Gap. Adelaida and Willow Creek were drawn up because of the fact that they are mainly on a calcareous formation. Willow Creek and Templeton Gap are influenced by this cool air coming through the Santa Lucia mountains. So those boundaries were clear.

HODGINS:

What do you like most about your winery's AVA, Willow Creek?

SMITH:

To me, Willow Creek has the perfect combination: the good soils of Adelaida and the good temperature variation of Templeton Gap. So it's like the ideal in-between.

It's a little bit warmer than most of Willow Creek, but it has the same soils. In Templeton Gap, the soil is mainly alluvial. And although alluvial does some great stuff, for me, calcareous soil is where it's at. It holds the acid better, which when you're dealing with these big, warm-climate varieties, like syrah and grenache, having that great acidity is really what makes our wines so big and ripe and rich. They also have this nice brightness that most wines that are ripe and rich don't have. Good brightness and nice, fresh acidity: in a nutshell, that's what makes Willow Creek special.

HODGINS:

I read that the vines' roots here tend to go deeper.

SMITH:

Exactly. It's all this fractured rock. The vines get their roots into those cracks and they dive down, follow the moisture and draw up the tasty goodness that lives there. Calcareous soils are very light and fluffy; they're pretty much like little sponges. We get a good amount of rainfall here, about 25 to 30 inches per year is the average, but it's all in the wintertime. What is so cool about these soils is that they grab all that winter moisture and hold onto it.

▼

The vines are able to suck that moisture back out throughout the summertime. It really helps moderate our heat by always having that moisture available. If you're planted in a looser, dryer, freer-draining soil, you have to rely on irrigation all the time to keep the grapes happy.

HODGINS:

You're a big believer in unusual blends as well as traditional ones.

SMITH:

I wouldn't want to see Paso turn too far towards cabernet. I think for one, it's no use competing with Napa; you're always going to be playing second fiddle. I always encourage people, even if they love cab, to at least play with some other stuff to bring it into a blend. That's the Paso way.

HODGINS:

How have wine consumers' tastes changed since you started making wine?

▼

SMITH:

It's exciting to see the generational shift. Younger people, their taste is so much broader than tastes were 30 years ago. It used to be that wine drinkers had to be told, "This is good, and this is what you should like." Now it's such a diverse world, so many different wines and flavors, and more access to different cuisines and cultures. I think the new generation of consumers are open to just a myriad of flavors.

▼

WINE TASTER'S LOG

📅 Date of visit:

_____

🍷 Wines tasted:

_____   _____

_____   _____

📋 Notes:

_____

_____

_____

I met Justin Smith and got his autograph!

_____

Justin Smith

SHARE YOUR VISIT WITH US ON INSTAGRAM!

#DriveThroughPasoRobles
@Drive_Through_Books
@ilikethisgrape

▼

—

FAQs ABOUT WINE TASTING

WINE TASTING CAN BE A BIT INTIMIDATING. RELAX! PASO IS A CASUAL AND FRIENDLY PLACE WHERE YOU'LL ALWAYS FEEL AT HOME. HERE ARE A FEW ANSWERS TO SOME COMMON QUESTIONS.

SHOULD I TIP?

Tipping isn't necessary, although you're welcome to do so if you feel you've gotten an extraordinary experience. Think of the tasting room staff as experts sharing their knowledge, not servers.

HOW MUCH TIME SHOULD I SPEND AT EACH WINERY?

It can vary according to the number of wines being offered and the way the tasting is structured. Generally it's more pleasurable to linger a bit — take in the beauty of your surroundings, sit outside near the vineyard if that's possible, and enjoy the overall experience. Wine is a great companion to social occasions and prompts many great conversations, often with strangers. You never know who you'll meet.

HOW MANY WINE TASTINGS A DAY IS OPTIMAL?

Don't rush! It's possible in parts of the region to visit many wineries in a day, but your experience is about more than simply drinking wine. Touring any wine region is definitely a "slow down and smell the roses" kind of pleasure. A number we like is three in a day.

IS IT RUDE TO ASK FOR A NEW GLASS EACH TIME I TRY A NEW WINE?

Glasses are often rinsed between tastings: a little dash of wine will be poured into your empty glass. Swish it around then dump it. If you're moving from white to red, you will sometimes be offered a fresh glass.

WHAT'S THE BEST WAY TO CLEAN MY PALATE BEFORE TRYING THE NEXT WINE?

You'll often find crackers or some other neutralizing food on the bar in tasting rooms for that purpose. Also, don't forget to swirl, sniff, sip and spit or dump. The less wine you drink, the sharper you and your palate will remain.

▼

IS IT RUDE NOT TO BUY ANY BOTTLES AFTER TASTING?

You're not obligated to buy anything, although many tasting rooms offer a discount such as a waived tasting fee when you buy.

WHAT IS THE BEST WAY TO TRAVEL BETWEEN WINERIES?

The gold standard is a large, comfortable hired vehicle with a knowledgeable driver, and there are several excellent tour operators in the Paso region. Uber and other services can get expensive. If you're in your own car, wine tasting with a designated driver is the best way to go.

BIBLIO-GRAPHY

California History. Quarterly publication. University of California Press.

Kroeber, A.L., *Handbook of the Indians of California*. Dover Publications, 2012.

Paso Robles Historical Society Virginia Peterson Research Library.

Paso Roble Wine Country Alliance. pasowine.com

Rice, Thomas J. and Tracy G. Cervellone, *Paso Robles: An American Terroir*. Self-published, 2007.

Starr, Kevin. *California: A History*. Random House, 2005.

Wine History Project of San Luis Obispo County. winehistoryproject.org

PAUL HODGINS

Paul Hodgins earned a doctorate in music from the University of Southern California and was a professor of dance at UC Irvine before switching careers to journalism, where his arts reviews and wine writing have won several awards and honors. Paul's book, *The Winemakers of Paso Robles*, was published in 2017.

KATHY LAJVARDI

Award-winning creative director, artist, designer Kathy Lajvardi graduated from Otis College of Art and Design and found immediate success in advertising, film and entertainment. She has worked with Madonna and Beyonce, and her graphics have appeared in movie trailers for Iron Man and Transformers. Her paintings and photographs have been featured at a dozen major galleries including NFTs. kathylajvardi.com

NAUSHAD HUDA

Chicago native residing in California. Naushad's day time is spent as a Director of Strategy for a global technology & consumer brands, and at night he's the founder of I Like This Grape whose mission is to make wine relatable to millennial audiences through unique wine events & publishing the Drive Through series of books. naushad@ilikethisgrape.com

OTHER BOOKS IN OUR *DRIVE THROUGH*™ SERIES

DRIVE THROUGH

DRIVE THROUGH™
NAPA

YOUR ULTIMATE COMPANION TO NAPA VALLEY'S WINE REGIONS

BUY IT NOW ON AMAZON
or SCAN THE QR CODE

"This book is an answer to dry guidebooks and stiff informational publications that pervade the wine industry."

– L.A. Times